The New City Gardener

The
New City
Gardener

Natural techniques and necessary skills for a successful urban garden

Judith Adam

with photographs by **Tim Saunders**

FIREFLY BOOKS

A FIREFLY BOOK

Published by Firefly Books Ltd. 1999

Copyright © 1999 Denise Schon Books Inc.
Text copyright © 1999 Judith Adam
Photographs copyright © 1999 Tim Saunders
A Denise Schon Book

Cataloguing-in-Publication Data

Adam, Judith

The new city gardener: natural techniques & necessary skills
for a successful urban garden

Includes index.

ISBN 1-55209-313-1

1. Gardening.   2. Gardens – Design.   I. Title.

SB453.A32   1998   635   C98-932618-7

Published in Canada in 1999
by Firefly Books Ltd.
3680 Victoria Park Avenue
Willowdale, Ontario
Canada M2H 3K1

Published in the United States in 1999
by Firefly Books (U.S.) Inc.
P.O. Box 1338, Ellicott Station
Buffalo, New York
USA 14205

Design: Counterpunch / Linda Gustafson
Editor: Jennifer Glossop
Production: Denise Schon Books Inc.
Index: Barbara Schon

Additional photography: "Before" photos on p.27 and
p.36 courtesy Judith Adam.

Printed and bound in Canada

*The publisher acknowledges the financial support of the
Government of Canada through the Book Publishing
Industry Development Program for its publishing activities.*

For Mary and Douglas Hart,
true gardeners, true friends.

Acknowledgments

Many thanks to Denise Schon, Anna Barron and Eva Quan for their unbridled optimism; to Tim Saunders for a special way of seeing; to Linda Gustafson, Peter Ross and Sue Meggs-Becker at Counterpunch for making the pages sing; to Susan Dyer and Jim Edmond for driving the idea; and to Stephen Westcott-Gratton for on-call research. Much appreciation to everyone who allowed us to photograph inside their garden gates; and to Tracy Estey, Julie Albert, Helen Hayes and Raymonde Donohue for keeping me in line. A special thank you to the Worek family for inviting me into their garden. And gratitude beyond measure to Marc, who shares the car with a gardener in dirty boots.

Contents

Preface

My first garden was in New York City. Clay pots on the fire escape outside my fifth-floor window grew yellow crookneck squash and cucumber vines. These prodigious growers needed little encouragement and quickly climbed up to the seventh floor. It was quite an aerial act to harvest them, but a good way to meet my neighbors!

City gardening requires a resourceful approach, and *The New City Gardener* offers information and techniques to make plants flourish in tough city conditions. In the past decade much of my work as a horticulturist and gardening lecturer and teacher has been answering questions and teaching people about gardening in the city. Those questions guided me in writing this book, and I hope it will give friendly reassurance to new and experienced garden makers. It seems gardeners are always beginning anew, and that, I'm sure, is why they live forever.

When I design and install gardens for my clients I try to understand their personal vision of the outdoor space and how the garden will be used. Gardens are private places, and my role is to interpret the owner's ideas in the materials at hand: soil, plants, water and stone. These are the building materials common to every garden site; only the dreams are different.

Garden making is a practical pursuit, but one often enhanced by imagination and memory. My own garden is influenced by summers spent with my grandmother at Rosemont Cottage on Absecon Island, off the southern coast of New Jersey. She was a church minister's wife with scarce time for planting, but the garden there had a life of its own and wanted little care. It was a place of abundant growth, with fuzzy green peaches falling prematurely from crowded branches and brilliant blue hydrangeas feeding off the acidic soil. This was a garden of many vines, of honeysuckle, tomatoes and self-seeded squash roaming the paths, and the encircling canes of grapes left to their own devices. And of course there were roses, the sweet and heavy scent of 'New Dawn' and 'Frühlingsgold' carried by ocean breezes into my bedroom at night. I took the garden quite for granted, and directed my interest to stalking feral cats who hid their kittens deep in the patches of mint and daylilies.

I hope this book will help you to recognize the character of soil and moisture in your own growing space, and the methods of giving plants what they need to grow in those conditions. Selecting plants that have the ability to thrive in dry or wet soils and light or shady places puts you halfway toward successful gardening. The other half is skill and resourcefulness, and these come in their own time. The process of gardening is its own reward, and connects us all to the natural world. There is always something important to do in city life, but I'd rather be in the garden.

Judith Adam
December 1998

Previous page: Impromptu plants soften the edges of this backdoor deck and patio. Sometimes what grows best in city conditions are the volunteer seedlings of perennials, spontaneously taking hold in cracks between paving stones. Their tenacious grip on the soil beneath the city is all the encouragement a gardener needs to reclaim the garden and get planting.

The New City Gardener

Introduction

New city gardening

The urban garden is found wherever it breaks through the cracks in city surfaces. Spontaneous, impetuous and irrepressible, the garden beneath the city resists the best efforts of construction technology to hold it back. Blades of wild grass and opportunistic trees shooting from masonry crevices are the everyday inspiration for city gardeners with their own private patch and a desire to tap the energies in the soil below street level.

Every city is built over a garden of green indigenous plants, although this is difficult to believe when you are standing on a street crowded with cars, apartment buildings and storefronts. The office towers of Toronto stand over a cleared Carolinian forest of dogwood and oak; Washington, D.C., is built over a wetland of alder and swamp maple; and the industrial sprawl of Chicago belies its civic motto, *Urbes In Horto*, city in a garden.

Pioneering city founders pursued development at the expense of plants flourishing on the site. Times change, and contemporary city gardeners are pioneers at putting plants back. With a motto of No Space Is Too Small, gardeners are picking holes in the city infrastructure and planting right down to the sidewalk.

This book is about city gardening and the challenge of growing in urban spaces. Often city gardening circumstances are more extreme than in suburbs or rural areas, although the basic gardening techniques are similar. Dry or wet compacted soil, deep shade or relentless sun are some of the conditions encountered when attempting to make a gar-

den from an abused backyard. Understanding the soil, moisture and light conditions of the site is the first step toward making intelligent design and planting decisions. Selecting adaptable plants and providing adequate care are the immediate goals in creating a garden that thrives and endures.

Time, the most important element required in making a garden, is chronically in short supply. The priority of city schedules is to get on, get through, get ahead. But gardeners can revise the pattern of days and reclaim extended hours of pleasure while making a personal landscape on a city lot. The best advice is *carpe diem*, seize the day.

Previous page: A small garden corner illustrates the serendipity of natural elements: wood, stone, gravel and water combine with grasses and conifers in a setting of rustic elegance.

Being in the garden doesn't always mean work. Thoughtful contemplation is as necessary to garden making as a strong spade and fertile soil. A place to sit and engage with the process invites an assessment of change through the growing season. Even winter plans for spring work projects are best considered 'in situ', outdoors and on the scene.

One

Garden style

Whose garden is this?

The idealized landscapes pictured in coffee-table books and design magazines inspire both an urge to make a beautiful garden and a fear that our efforts won't measure up to the glossy photos. This dilemma can disarm even the best gardening efforts.

Rather than lose another season to indecision, put aside the pictures of other people's gardens and step into your own for an honest consideration of how you would like it to be. The seductive lure of elaborate English perennial borders and sparsely elegant Japanese courtyards are both visions of delight, but do you want them for your own? Following the complex planting charts of gardening masters at best provides you with borrowed artwork. These are illustrations drawn by other hands, reflecting priorities and sensibilities not our own. Without doubt, they are aesthetically chosen and professionally executed, but they lack the insight and inspiration of your own discovery. Knowing what is comforting, interesting and rewarding for you can be difficult to determine when you are presented with too many gardening choices and a limited opportunity to develop an individual style.

Gardens are personal places, likely to be viewed by invitation only. Those peeking over the fence are welcome to the treasures they may view, but these are entirely stolen moments. Making a garden is a rare license to create the world as you would have it, to reflect your temperament and philosophy in the landscape you call your own. Gardens grow, mature and change along with the peo-

Previous page: An arched door frame invites the busy and eclectic planting of a cottage garden. Clusters of roses, hollyhocks, lilies and Japanese anemones swell throughout the beds on each side of the front door, and steps are bordered with containers of annual plants. Ivy cascades over the door frame and across the stone step risers as the garden assumes a dominant role in the presentation of this entrance.

ple who make them, and this evolution generates many rewards as seasons pass.

The easiest and sometimes most revealing way to learn your own preferences is to evaluate the manner in which you organize personal areas such as desk drawers, sewing baskets, toolboxes and bathroom cabinets. These areas usually reflect your natural style expressed without inhibition. A great deal can be learned about your stylistic preference by the state of your underwear drawer, or how many pieces of silverware you use to set a table. Carefully organized closets with everything in place translate to a more structured garden style, with formal entrances and seating areas, balanced borders and plants chosen for their stately form and well-defined lines. Boxwood hedges, for example, would make good space organizers in such a garden, along with standard rose trees and stone urns. Drawers in which the contents are disorganized translate into a relaxed garden setting, with naturalized areas of mixed perennial plantings and cascading shrubs. This informal garden might have collections of large hostas under Japanese maples, an area for spring bloodroot, bleeding hearts, primulas and forget-me-nots, of lilac, hydrangea and mock orange shrubs.

The question to ask is not so much what you want, but rather what rewards and gratifies you? What kind of environment makes you feel secure, able to relax? What balance of order and chaos centers your thoughts? What forms, textures and colors are consistently pleasing? Gardens we make ourselves are hopefully in our own image, our own profile expressed in a handmade living landscape. A bit of self-obsession doesn't go amiss in the garden.

User-friendly gardens

More than a few gardeners dream of rose arbors and peony splendors, only to be brought rudely to earth by the rough justice of a backyard football squad. First and most essential, consider who uses the garden and for what purpose. If children with play equipment and kiddy pools are part of the action, be sure to factor them into the plan. Sharing the space is important to the democratic process of families, and children will quickly make their own connections to the natural world when their activities are welcome and planned for.

Planning a city garden always begins with an acknowledgment of how the space will meet its users' needs. Rather than impose restrictions by forbidding football or eliminating the raspberry patch, build these uses into the plan. Thoughtful consideration of the space will include the needs of every user and a combination of all interests. Some compromise may be necessary, but you win respect and a lot of points for this negotiation. These are chips you can cash in down the road when your expanding planting beds begin to infringe on the lawn.

If the whole family has an interest in using garden space for individual purposes, it may be necessary to take advantage of both front and back garden areas. Horticultural goings-on can be separated from ball and net games by putting the athletic activities in the front garden. All children know that basketball is the second-most important use of a driveway. A low fence or hedge may be necessary to keep players and equipment in bounds yet still allow passers-by to gather and enjoy the game.

The interests of flower growers and vegetable growers can be negotiated with great charm in a cottage garden planting. Combining shasta daisies and delphiniums with tomatoes and currants appeals to all the senses. Almost every perennial plant and flowering shrub pairs well with food plants chosen

User survey

There is a time and a place for everyone's interests in the garden. These are some of the choices:

Perennial plant beds
Roses
Flowering shrubs
Flowering vines
Rock garden
Scree or gravel garden
Trough gardens
Bog garden
Container garden
Herb garden
Cutting garden
Wildflower patch
Lawn
Ornamental pond
Vegetable patch

Berry canes
Dwarf fruit trees
Seating in sun
Seating in shade
Eating area, table and chairs
Garage
Storage shed
Swimming pool
Sand box
Kiddy pool
Swings and climbing set
Tricycle path
Athletic games
Drying laundry

for their attractive display. Purpleleaf sand cherry with ruby Swiss chard at its feet, bleeding heart with a skirt of Italian 'Lolla Rossa' lettuce, and hydrangea flanked with red pear tomatoes are some of the colorful combinations of mixed plantings.

Privacy and retreat are also important user needs to be considered. A quiet place for reading and the occasional nap should always be available. Building in a small seating place at the back of the garden to accommodate a bench or two chairs will give you a reason to stop work and enjoy the view of your favorite plants. Even a hammock strung between two trees is an opportunity to simply enjoy being in the garden with no particular task at hand except contemplation of the sky.

Developing a profile

Discussions of garden style can be esoteric to the point of exhaustion. But it's simple to understand style as a sliding scale of orderly arrangement, starting with a rigid placement of plants in formal beds surrounded by hard surface areas, moving to a more relaxed arrangement of seating areas with lawns bordered by drifts of plants flowing into each other, and ending with a completely natural and unstructured landscape of wildflowers, shrubs and trees spontaneously appearing in the garden. If making landscape decisions brings on a serious anxiety attack, you might start with one corner or area, developing a

Style indicators

Interest in particular features can help to determine garden style.

Formal	*Relaxed*	*Naturalized*
Balanced design	Asymmetrical design	Unstructured design
French parterre	Perennial border	Herbs and grasses
Stone terrace	Brick patio	Stepping stones
Square-cut flagstone	Mossy limestone	Pea gravel
Boundary beds	Island beds	Drifts and areas
Topiary specimens	Shrub roses	Wildflowers
Raised bed	Berm	Hillside
Wall fountain	Bird bath	Dry stream bed
Reflecting pool	Pond	Bog
Statuary	Arbor	Sundial
Peacocks	Goldfish	Rabbits
Tulip	Primula	Trillium
Laburnum	Lilac	Dogwood
Alleys	Walkways	Paths

A relaxed cottage-garden style on a city lot allows for maximum use of plants in a small space. Houseplants summering outdoors flourish alongside annuals, perennials and vines under the canopy of mature city trees. Self-seeded plants pop up in beds and paving cracks and are allowed to blossom where they take hold. The homemade pond is stocked with fish, tadpoles and water lilies and brings the sound of a small cascade to the garden. Eliminating most of the lawn means the 30-foot width of the garden can accommodate planting beds, pond, seating areas and storage shed. Allowing vines to grow on fences and the shed incorporates these structures into the garden. Most plant maintenance takes place in spring and autumn, with weekly deadheading during the summer season. Despite the naturalized setting, the subway is just down the street.

The practical directive of a straight path is offset by massing ground covers and diversions along the way. Granite boulders are installed to appear as if emerging from the earth, and a bird bath set amongst large pebbles is a natural stopping place. The sundial and reflective gazing ball in the garden rooms behind focus attention into the center of these small areas.

prototype of style that you can eventually extend throughout the garden. Because gardening mistakes are as common as successes, this plan also limits the damage to a small area. Working from one area to another, the garden will evolve more comfortably, and perhaps with greater reward.

Your style choice should also complement your circumstances. Formal Georgian architecture is seldom enhanced by a front-yard wildflower meadow. Similarly, a board-and-batten country chalet would be at war with a cut-stone terrace and boxwood topiary. The key factor is a sympathetic relationship between your house and your garden, inviting a reassuring similarity of character and design. For example, a tall and narrow Victorian row house is best complemented by busy borders of cottage garden flowers and billowing shrubs, and an ultramodern structure is suited to hardwood plants with clearly defined lines.

The plants that spontaneously appeal to you, like a graceful tree for the front lawn or a luxuriant weeping shrub in the border, are also good indicators of your personal style. And interesting things can result from a mix-and-match collection of features, something like setting the dinner table with unmatched but intrinsically charming patterns. Using a well-chosen and unexpected plant, like a sensuously flowing Walker's cut-leaf caragana in a bed of stiff dwarf evergreens, can add just a bit of contrast and personality to a setting.

Massing Ground Covers

Alpine strawberry, *Fragaria vesca,* zone 4, sun to shade
Barrenwort, *Epimedium* spp., zone 4, shade
Bearberry cotoneaster, *Cotoneaster dammeri,* zone 4, sun
Bishop's weed, *Aegopodium podograria,* zone 3, sun to shade, invasive
Bugleweed, *Ajuga reptans,* zone 3, sun to shade
Chameleon plant, *Houttuynia cordata,* zone 6, sun to shade, invasive
Cranesbill, *Geranium* x *oxonianum* 'Claridge Druce', zone 4, sun
Cranesbill, *Geranium macrorrhizum* 'Bevan's Variety', zone 3, sun to shade
Creeping jenny, *Lysimachia nummularia,* zone 3, sun
Creeping juniper hybrids, *Juniperus horizontalis,* zone 3, sun

Creeping thyme, *Thymus* spp., zone 4, sun
Daylilies, *Hemerocallis* hybrids, zone 3, sun
Foamflower, *Tiarella cordifolia,* zone 3, sun to shade
Japanese spurge, *Pachysandra terminalis,* zone 3, sun to shade
Lamb's-ears, *Stachys byzantina,* zone 4, sun
Lily-of-the-valley, *Convallaria majalis,* zone 3, shade
Moss phlox, *Phlox subulata,* zone 3, sun
Perennial candytuft, *Iberis sempervirens,* zone 3, sun
Plantain lily, *Hosta* spp., zone 3, sun to shade
Siberian carpet cypress, *Microbiota decussata,* zone 3, sun to shade
Sweet woodruff, *Galium odoratum,* zone 3, shade
Wild ginger, *Asarum canadense,* zone 2, shade

Time check: how much do you have?

Sometimes city gardeners are hard pressed to be reasonable, particularly when they urgently need to establish a green buffer against surrounding buildings. The first scent of newly thawed earth in spring often generates plans of great dimension. That is all very well, but to implement grand plans, time and energy must also be available on an exuberant scale. When making decisions about style, design and garden layout, it's important to evaluate the maintenance needs as well as the initial installation. In other words, how often can you get your hands dirty?

For example, beds for perennial or annual flowers, although lovely, are labor-intensive and require frequent weeding. It is an absolute fact that weeds grow faster than gardeners can crawl, and quite a bit of time will be spent on hands and knees pulling them out. Garden folklore says it takes seven years of persistent cultivation to rid the soil's top layer of weed seeds. But of course, every turn of the trowel brings more seeds to the surface.

Covering the soil between plants with an organic mulch is an effective way to prevent weeds from growing. Organic materials such as shredded leaves and shredded bark are very efficient at suppressing weed growth and also slowly degrade into plant food. Wood chips are often used, but degrade more unevenly and are most appropriate under shrubs and trees.

To block sunlight, organic materials must be 2 to 3 inches (5 to 7.5 cm) in thickness. This may seem unusually generous, but that is what it takes to prevent weed seeds from germinating. Although the mulch may appear quite thick, it will sink quickly.

A more interesting choice is to use ground-cover plants with densely massing growth patterns to prevent weed growth. The key to their success is planting them closely for quick filling in, and providing manure and frequent watering for speedy growth during their first season. If groundcover plants are well cared for the entire first season, they will mass together rapidly. But until that happens, even the ground cover will need to be weeded or mulched.

*Like the course of true love, a good path seldom runs straight. A simple path of random stepping stones is given character by the slightly swaying line that allows perennial flowers to spill forward and conceal the destination. A stray Italian white sunflower bobs over the purple coneflowers (*Echinacea purpurea*), black-eyed Susan (*Rudbekia spp.*) and bouncing bet (*Saponaria officinalis*), and the end of the line is marked by a singular cedar.*

Garden layout: sizing up the situation

When you are planning extensive changes to an outdoor area, it's useful to have an accurate scale drawing of the site. Knowing the exact dimensions of your available spaces ensures that plants will be placed where they have sufficient room to grow to maturity.

Begin by noting important information on a large sheet of graph paper. Include the scale, such as ¼ inch = 1 foot (1:50); an arrow pointing to north; a description of the site, such as "bed by kitchen door, with storage shed" and the date. For a drawing of the entire site, the first measurement to take is the lot size. When the boundaries of your lot are drawn onto the graph paper, a corner of the house can be placed on the lot by measuring its distance from the two closest lot lines. Then measure the length of front, back and side walls to place the house on the chart. Other significant features to be added are patios and other hard-surfaced areas, garage or shed, swimming pool, ponds and bird baths, walkways and steps, large trees and shrubs, and existing flower beds. Also write down any pertinent information such as areas of full sun or deep shade, difficult soil conditions or poor drainage, neighboring structures or trees that may affect the site, advantageous views or ghastly sights.

You may want to keep the master drawing

as a reference and make a copy for revisions and for noting existing plants and plants to be purchased. Where construction of features, like a deck or pathway, is planned, indicate the type of stone, paver or wood to be used. A drawing that is loaded with information and tattered about the edges is the hallmark of an enthusiastic gardener!

Garden bones: starting out with trees

The best time to consider the merits of garden structure is in February, when foliage is absent and no floriferous distractions are flaunting themselves about the place. This is the mo-

A rental strategy

The renter-gardener walks a fine line. How much liberty can you take with the garden without causing your landlord to be concerned over the deliveries of soil and sand? It is always better to be up front about these things. Mention an interest in "dabbling in flowers" and offer an assurance that you won't be making any major structural changes.

Working in a rented garden is a good exercise in making the best of a situation. Having to accept whatever light is available can lead to a thorough education in what plants will grow well in those conditions. Soil improvement is certainly possible, and there is no reason to expect anything other than success. Certainly perennial, annual and vegetable plants can be grown, but an interest in shrubs and trees might be better directed to large containers. This method will avoid any major disruption of the rented premises and also make it possible to move these big-ticket items when the lease is up.

ment of truth and cold light, when what you see is what you get. The displays of spring, summer and autumn are long gone, and what remains is the bare bones of structure and form, the woody underpinning that supports the production of so many seasonal pleasures.

In cities much "negative structure" exists in surrounding walls, street signs and utility poles. Trees can help to distract attention from these intruding forms. Large plants with permanent woody structures are the bones that give a garden shape and presence when placed in prominent locations. Evergreen trees and shrubs are also key components and provide much diversity of color and texture in the bleak winter months.

When selecting trees and shrubs for structural purpose, look for clearly definable lines and shapes. Trees like English oaks have strong vertical lines, flowering dogwoods have tiered horizontal layers of branches, and evergreen Serbian spruce has graceful drooping branches. Other plants, such as lilacs, are more disorganized in their limb structure and don't have enough year-round style to be prominent structural plants.

Smaller plants can also make good garden bones if they have clear lines. Dwarf Alberta spruce is a small, cone-shaped evergreen with deep green color in winter, and 'Mint Julep' juniper is a dwarf evergreen with outward-thrusting branches that make strong features when planted in small groups. Even the consistency of a low boxwood hedge can provide a structural influence when it's used to define the shape of a pathway or planting bed.

Before and after

Interior home renovation made quite a mess in the front garden of the Victorian-era row house. Dumpster bins and building materials are cleared away, but what remains (right) is less than gracious. A new slightly swayed walkway of tumbled cobblestones (below) helps to make this very narrow lot appear wider. Ornamental pear trees on the left buffer the condominium entrance next door, and a ground cover lawn of periwinkle is an attractive feature in all seasons.

Placing trees: the biggest garden bones

Traditional theory suggests that the tallest and largest plant structures should be placed farthest from the house. This concept puts big trees in the far corners where they can find a bit of room to spread and fill the ninety-degree angles. Of course, there are always opportunities to break rules, and if the tree is tall and skinny, like 'Purple Fountain' weeping

A small pond becomes more than a water feature when it recreates natural history using mossy rocks and plants with year-round presence. A weeping lace-leaf Japanese maple (Acer palmatum dissectum spp.) at the highest point enhances the elevation and emulates the gently cascading water below. Against a background of cedar and rhododendron, dwarf conifers including hemlock (Tsuga canadensis 'Jeddeloh', zone 4), Hinoki false cypress (Chamaecyparis obtusa 'Nana Gracilis', zone 5) and Mugho pine (Pinus mugo var. pumilio, zone 2) provide four-season naturalism. Ornamental grasses and perennials are features in warm months, and snow embellishes the rocks in winter. Elevating one side of the pond with piled rocks invites water to cascade with the aid of the recirculating pump and plastic tubing. Even a simple elevation of 8 to 12 inches will give a pond greater interest and dimension in a small space.

Organizing the big projects

Constructing a garden bed, making a small pond or moving mountains of soil requires lots of muscle and many hours. Planning is essential, and so is an accurate estimation of the time and resources required for each section of a large project. Small successes are very important and provide the reward every gardener deserves. Satisfaction grows by planning work that can be completed within the season, with time to spare for enjoying the fruits of labor.

- Select a section of the garden for major construction work such as building a fence, small pond, new planting bed or patio. Don't attempt to accomplish a complete garden makeover in one season.

- Do the research, and be clear on all details of plant choice and material construction. Locate sources and identify costs for all materials and equipment in advance. Avoid any unplanned or impulse expenditures, and assemble all materials on the site before starting work.

- Assign projects to gardening helpers and get their commitment to complete the job. Offer quality inducements and great treats!

- Make sure a full day or a series of days is available for the work and will not be interrupted by other demands. Leave portable telephones inside. Have hot or cold drinks handy, plan to order in food, and don't do any laundry until the end. Select a raindate just in case.

- Have a camera handy to document the progress of work from start to finish. This will be a valuable record of your work, and an opportunity to show friends how it's done.

- Be sure to schedule leisure time after completion to enjoy the finished project, and invite friends – and those helpers – in to admire your success.

beech (*Fagus sylvatica* 'Purple Fountain', zone 6, height 18 feet (5.5 m), spread 8 feet (2.4 m), it can easily be accommodated at the corner of a two-story home where it will soften the sharp angle of the building. Big trees for the corners of city lots can be very tall, but must have a slender girth so they won't overwhelm nearby plants. Good choices include Korean fir (*Abies koreana*, zone 4, height 30 feet (9 m), spread 12 feet (3.5 m) and Swiss stone pine (*Pinus cembra*, zone 2, height 30 feet (9 m), spread 8 feet (2.4 m). Both are slow-growing evergreen plants with good winter color and interesting texture and will adapt their forms to corner locations. Comparable tall and narrow deciduous trees include columnar maple (*Acer platanoides* 'Columnare', zone 5, height 36 feet (11 m), spread 12 feet (3.5 m) and cutleaf mountain ash (*Sorbus aucuparia* 'Asplenifolia', zone 2, height 36 feet (11 m), spread 8 feet (2.4 m), which produces the classic red-orange berries of this family.

Narrow city lots can spare little space for spreading trees. Slender conifers like black cedar (*Thuja occidentalis* 'Nigra', zone 3, height 15 feet (4.5 m), spread 4 feet (1.2 m) work well in corners, as do 'Wichita Blue' juniper and 'Springbank' juniper (*Juniperus scopulorum* 'Wichita Blue' and 'Springbank', zone 4, height 12 feet (3.5 m), spread 4 feet (1.2 m). Another choice with more open form and attractive berries is 'Fairview' juniper (*J. chinensis* 'Fairview', zone 5, height 12 feet (3.5 m), spread 3 feet (90 cm).

Planting trees as structural elements in open areas of lawn calls for a bit of judgment and for smaller-scale plants. Lawn trees often look just fine when first planted but as they grow they may dominate the house and the garden. Consider a tree's ultimate scale before you buy it. Dense coniferous trees with a substantial mass of branches ideally should grow no taller than the house and not be placed where they will block access to doors and windows. A good choice for silvery-blue color and year-round interest is 'Fat Albert' spruce (*Picea pungens* 'Fat Albert', zone 3, height 15 feet (4.5 m), spread 8 feet (2.4 m), a strong structural element with classic ascending form and slow, controlled growth.

Tall trees can be placed in lawns if they are sufficiently delicate in structure and have an open branching pattern, thereby allowing light in. Good choices are the standard trunk-form of serviceberry (*Amelanchier canadensis*, zone 4, height 24 feet (9 m), spread 8 feet (2.4 m) and its hybrid cousins with larger flowers, 'Ballerina' serviceberry and 'Apple' serviceberry. All of the serviceberries are small-leafed and have attractive light gray bark, charming white flowers in spring followed by litter-less dark blue berries, and brilliant color in autumn. Another highly ornamental choice is river birch (*Betula nigra*, zone 4, height 36 feet (11 m), spread 20 feet (6 m), with tan to salmon-pink shaggy, exfoliating bark and delicately ascending branches. The river birch has strong golden color in autumn and is resistant to wood-boring insects.

Lot lines: useful city structures

Lot lines are rigid forms imposed on city gardens, and there is seldom anything graceful about them. But they do delineate the property and act as a border for the private space within. In city gardens, lot lines are almost always marked by fences or hedges.

When planning a new fence or hedge, it makes sense to set the structure slightly inside the surveyed line to be sure of ownership and control: it is universally unacceptable to poke another man's fire, but to meddle with his hedge is possible if it's planted directly on a shared lot line.

Dense cedar hedges give a sense of privacy and enclosure, but small gardens can be made to appear slightly wider with an open hedge or

The arbor and white picket fence of this cottage garden have been set behind the ornamental planting in a generous expression of openness. Presenting the garden in front of the fence offers it to public view and access, a gesture not often encountered in city gardens. Fences are clear indicators of what is private and public, and their placement will influence how the garden is perceived. The use of scented plants like roses and lavender is a further inducement for the passing public to stop and enjoy an extraordinary gift.

a staggered planting of low-growing orna-mental shrubs like dwarf lilac (*Syringa meyeri* or *S. velutina*, zone 3, height 5 feet (1.5 m), spread 5 feet (1.5 m), or dwarf American cranberry (*Viburnum trilobum* 'Compactum', zone 2, height 5 feet (1.5 m), spread 5 feet (1.5 m).

Doorsteps and corners

Houses without shrubs planted along their foundations always look as if they are floating in space and have only recently dropped from the sky. They need a foundation planting to anchor them visually on the lot. Woody plants at the doorstep and surrounding the house are important structural features that connect the building to the landscape and give context to the house. These plants are seen throughout the year, and their prominent location is sure to draw attention. Yet foundation plantings regularly slip into disarray, with plants growing either too spindly or too robust. The choices for this location must be made very carefully, using the criteria of eventual height and spread, and factoring in enough detail of color, form and texture to provide interest in four seasons.

Good choices for foundation planting include weeping white pine (*Pinus strobus* 'Pendula', zone 4, height 6 feet (1.8 m), spread 8 feet (2.4 m) and corkscrew hazel (*Corylus avellana* 'Contorta', zone 4, height 7 feet (2 m), spread 6 feet (1.8 m), both distinctive plants with cascading form. Smaller plants to com-

bine with them might be silvery-blue globe blue spruce (*Picea pungens* 'Glauca Globosa', zone 2, height 3 feet (90 cm), spread 4 feet (1.2 m) and 'Mountain Fire' pieris (*Pieris japonica* 'Mountain Fire', zone 6, height 4 feet (1.2 m), spread 4 feet (1.2 m), a broadleaf evergreen with small lustrous leaves and intense red new spring foliage.

Next to the doorstep is the perfect location for a plant with sufficient character to provide continuing interest as you come and go. A "specimen plant" is any plant with enough style to stand on its own, such as woody plants with graceful form and multiple ornamental features like blossoms, berries or handsome bark. Specimen plants can be placed to one side of the door and should be within human scale, 6 feet (1.8 m) or under. Small cascading trees like shade-tolerant weeping hemlock (*Tsuga canadensis* 'Pendula', zone 4) and sun-loving cutleaf weeping caragana (*Caragana arborescens* 'Walker', zone 2) are graceful forms to admire in passing.

Sometimes taller plants are appropriate near a residence. A tallish tree placed at an exposed corner will soften the angularity. This is a good place for a nice fat evergreen like 'Emerald' cedar (*Thuja occidentalis* 'Emerald', zone 4) or a dramatically weeping coniferous tree such as weeping Nootka false cypress (*Chamaecyparis nootkatensis* 'Pendula', zone 5) along with a splendid stone boulder to weep upon.

*Much can be made from the passage of a front walkway. The emphatic naturalism of ornamental grasses in flower, low-spreading conifers and Japanese maples imparts a casual elegance along the way to the front door. Massive stepping stones set into pea gravel strongly anchor this garden and formalize the lush display of plants against a forest background. The fine texture of the red lace-leaf Japanese maple (*Acer palmatum dissectum spp.*) confirms that form, texture and color are guiding principles in garden design.*

Areas and spaces

Reclaiming the garden

City gardeners share a common denominator: the arbitrary availability of gardening areas. The city, with its structures and surfaces and grids of development, takes little account of local terrain or of the soil quality and plant growth. Private gardens are low priority in city design and are relegated to whatever space is left undeveloped behind the house. The gap between the front door and the street is "the lawn," a no-man's-land of impersonal character where private and public properties meet. Narrow passages along the sides of the house are, at best, dismissed as service areas or, at worst, cemented over.

Clearly, a reappraisal is in order. Those who take pleasure in plants and a living landscape often need to transgress the accepted maxims of private-property use in this century. Even the most mild-mannered wielder of the trow-el eventually resorts to guerrilla-gardening tactics, chipping away at the city's infrastructure and liberating the soil. Concrete walks and asphalt driveways give way to drought-tolerant plantings of evening primrose (*Oenothera* spp.) and ornamental thymes (*Thymus* spp.), and forgotten sunny corners are reclaimed and nourished for the seductions of peonies and shrub roses.

Taking back the soil may distress one's more traditional neighbors. Redevelopment of the sacrosanct front lawn is so fraught with tension and fear of neighborly recrimination, it is often accomplished in the darkness of night. Come the dawn, there is the bold statement of one gardener's desire to interrupt the uniform profile of the city boulevard with an expression of whimsical design. However, it's usually best to let everyone know that this planting business is going to be up front and personal.

You may need more practical reasons for altering the city site to reassure your nongardening neighbors, and the dollar value of real estate may carry some weight. No one willingly writes off a dining room. Yet often sizable exterior spaces are disregarded despite their considerable square-foot land value. This is a reasonable and defensible argument to offer those who witness in stunned silence the removal of an unused and unsalvageable garage or storage shed. By liberating the land from disuse we gain back its value, along with the opportunity to realize new levels of appreciation from the urban garden.

Before and after

Enthusiastic gardeners are eager to take advantage of every vacant space. This unused stretch of lawn (right) alongside the house is 16 feet wide, and has been reclaimed for garden use by removing the grass and constructing a small stone patio surrounded with planting beds. Random flagstone (below) was used to reflect the informal setting, with stepping stone pathways on either side. Creeping ground covers, perennials and small flowering shrubs will eventually cover the soil. (The astute gardener has the rain down-spout hooked up to a collection barrel fitted with an access faucet on the side.) The two-seater bench makes this an inviting place for quiet moments.

Determining assets and deficits

Evaluating your garden's assets and how to further enhance them is usually a pleasure. Occasionally something of value has been inherited, perhaps a skillfully made dry-stone wall or a bed of antique roses. That wall could be gilded with cascading thyme and dianthus inserted into simple planting pockets. The rose bed might be bordered with a softening hedge of lavender or coral bells (*Heuchera* spp.). Sometimes the best asset is not entirely your own, such as a charming view across neighboring properties. No matter, take advantage of the fortuitous vista and plant slender trees or erect an arbor to frame the scene.

Deficits are another matter. Is there anything unspeakably ugly? If so, who owns it? Can it be removed, or must it be concealed in some way? It might be a large, nearly dead shrub or tree, an ancient shed giving shelter to wildlife or the oppressive side of a neighboring structure. Strategies for these problems are fairly straightforward. If a ghastly sight is situated on the other side of the fence, you can always attempt friendly negotiations to effect a mutually beneficial change, perhaps with shared expense for removal. But bear in mind that one gardener's weed might be another gardener's rose. Circumstances are sometimes nonnegotiable, and if the offending object is to remain in view, a distraction must be created.

Making unwanted objects disappear is a standard element of garden magic. One simple method is to provide a diversion for the eye. For example, a nearby plant of greater size and notable structure or coloring will minimize the dark and dead side of a large neighboring shrub. Keep in mind that the diversion must be sufficiently splendid to hold attention through more than one season. Characteristics like the shaggy bark of river birch (*Betula nigra*), the deep purple foliage of 'Bloodgood' Japanese maple (*Acer palmatum* 'Bloodgood') and the elegant texture of eastern hemlock (*Tsuga canadensis*) have considerable and lasting appeal. Ground covers with interesting foliage and flowers can be used to surround the diversion and clinch the attention-grabbing deal. Herbaceous perennial plants such as the cranesbill geraniums and felty gray-leafed lamb's-ears (*Stachys byzantina*) have aesthetic value from early spring until late autumn.

Concealment is sometimes the better part of gardening valor, and when confronted with an ugly brick wall along one side of the garden, the urge to wallpaper it over may be irresistible. This method of exterior decoration is accomplished with the aid of slender pyramidal trees planted shoulder-to-shoulder along the boundary line. (Plant hybridizers developed these narrow and straight hybrids of familiar, and larger, specimens.) Beech and mountain ash, ornamental pear and crab-

A love of plants requires a resourceful attitude about space. This gardener has gradually moved planting beds into the driveway, sacrificing garage access but gaining a cottage garden entrance to the gallery of roses behind. The garage has become an extraordinary vine-covered shape as Boston ivy (the kudzu of the north) makes its way across the garden.

apple, hornbeam and oak are all available in pyramidal form for use as living screens with great seasonal variety and appeal to birds as well as gardeners.

Dealing with deficits can bring out strong territorial instincts in gardeners. When the problem falls within your own venue and fenceline, direct and swift solutions are possible. If a miserable relic of shrub or tree offends the view, then have it out. The removal will be like the end of a toothache, followed by a sense of relief.

Shameless trickery

Politely put, some city gardens are more aesthetically challenged than others. These backyard ugly ducklings may be disadvantaged by closet-like dimensions, or bowling-alley shape, or a blankness rivaling that of a vacant parking lot. A bit of alteration and simple trickery can go a long way toward making wasted space into a pleasant garden.

SMALL SPACES

Small, claustrophobic gardens can be made to appear larger by establishing a subtle change in elevation. A slightly raised deck or stone patio area, perhaps only 2 or 3 inches (5 to 7.5 cm) above grade, is sufficient to create a distinct change in level. The smallness of the garden can be offset in the same way a large chair or cabinet is used to expand interior space in a small living room. Installing a slightly over-scale woody plant suggests a more expansive garden area. An ornamental shrub or tree with see-through delicate structure (such as a birch or laceleaf sumac) will allow light and air currents to pass through while still contributing architectural structure and an increased sense of size.

Another idea is to mount an exterior mirror on a wall and frame it with a trellis. The mirror creates the appearance of an entrance through the trellis and increases the perceived size of the garden. Reflected light from the mirror also enlarges the perceived space and brightness.

LONG AND NARROW SPACES

The tunnel effect in long, narrow city gardens can be broken up by staggered points of interest. A seating area of natural flagstone or paving bricks installed one-third of the way down the length of the garden, and a small pond or water feature surrounded by a copse of graceful shrubs and trees two-thirds of the way along the length, will stop the viewer's gaze from rushing immediately to the back wall. A connecting pathway of stepping stones set into grass can meander in a curved line between areas of interest. Flowering vines grown along the walls help to draw attention sideways and increase the perceived width.

SHORT AND NARROW SPACES

Short, narrow gardens can be made to appear wider and more evenly proportioned by arranging the space on a diagonal. Place a patio-seating area in one corner and a focal planting in the opposite diagonal corner. Including a strong architectural feature in the planting, such as a bird bath or piece of statuary, helps to link the diagonal corners, which in turn helps to broaden the narrow space and suggests a more graceful perspective in the limited area.

LARGE AND FLAT SPACES

Excessively large gardens may have a vacant and static appearance, particularly if there is no change in elevation. Their open, expansive

Making a planted berm

Choose a location for the berm, or gentle hill, that can be seen and enjoyed in all seasons. Use a rubber hose to outline a shape (a vinyl hose won't stay in place), either symmetrical or irregular, with curved edges and flowing lines. Berm plantings are so well appreciated that gardeners often wish they had been more generous in construction, so consider starting with a berm that's slightly larger than adequate.

If construction is on turf grass, layer eight thicknesses of newspaper over the outlined shape to smother the grass. Cover the newspaper with 12 inches (30 cm) of soil to accommodate planting perennials, and up to 24 inches (60 cm) of soil for the rootballs of shrubs. Contour the soil to achieve maximum height in the center, with a flat top and gently sloping sides.

If the berm is constructed in late autumn, cover it with leaves or a mulch of shredded bark. Rain and snow will cause the height to sink approximately a third. If construction is in spring, leave the berm uncovered and water it well with a sprinkler. Allow it to drain and settle for a week, and then install the plants. The berm will continue to sink gradually after planting.

look can be boring, especially when the space lacks organization or isn't delineated into interest areas. The garden can be divided into areas with the aid of low hedges or informal island beds; by changes in surface materials such as stone and groundcover plants, and by changes in elevation. Constructing a gentle hill, or berm, is an easy way to bring interest to a flat area. The berm can later be covered with turf grass or planted with low shrubs and perennial plants.

HILLS AND SLOPES

Moderately sloping ground has a sense of movement to it and can be an interesting garden area, but planting is difficult when the terrain is too steep. Everything wants to fall down the hill, and natural plant forms are distorted as gravity pulls them toward the

*By abandoning the idea of a lawn, it was possible to put this large berm on one side of a small city garden. Anchored at one end by a bird coliseum/ vine post and at the other by a weeping false cypress tree (*Chamaecyparis nootkatensis *'Pendula', zone 5), the berm is set with rocks to create informal planting areas and a sense of upper and lower tiers. The neighboring garage wall helps to anchor the berm in the landscape and is a backdrop to the progression of spring bulbs and perennial plants throughout the growing season.*

bottom. Slopes can be made more graceful by planting woody shrubs with naturally cascading forms, like weeping forsythia (*Forsythia suspensa*, zone 6) and lace-leaf Japanese maple (*Acer palmatum dissectum* spp., zone 5), both of which will adapt their form to the movement of the slope. If it is comfortable to walk on the slope, a pathway of natural stepping stones can cut through the downward movement and visit select plantings. Small trees with open branch structure, such as pagoda dogwood (*Cornus alternifolia*, zone 4) and eastern redbud (*Cercis canadensis*, zone 6), provide vertical lines to break up the downward movement of steep hills, and they can be set into the slope approximately every 20 feet (6 m). If planting is difficult because of the steep terrain, set boulders into the hill to create natural stone outcroppings with just enough level soil to accommodate the tree's root ball.

Plants in pots

Containers of all kinds can be used for growing plants. But whatever you choose, an old shoe or antique urn, the container must have drainage holes in the bottom. Without a way for excess water to drain away the plants will quickly succumb to oxygen deprivation. Decorative containers without drainage can be used if the plant is in a standard pot with holes and then set into the larger container.

Plastic pots are ideal for maintaining consistent moisture in the soil, but terra-cotta pots are the choice of many gardeners. Clay is a porous material, allowing air to penetrate the soil mass and supply the roots with plenty of oxygen. In the heat of summer, daily watering may be necessary. However, you can have the pleasure of clay pots without the daily watering by lining them with plastic. Cut a hole in the bottom of a plastic bag that comfortably fits the container and push it down into the pot. Fill with soil mix, cut off the excess plastic and install your plants. This method also works well with decorative baskets and fruit crates.

There are as many potting soil mixtures as there are biscuit recipes. Find one that you like and stick with it. Soilless mixes sold for pots are peat-based and generally don't contain any nutrients, although they do hold water well. You will have to supply all the plant food. A mixture of half soilless mix and half compost will hold moisture and provide some nutrition. You can use either your own garden compost or aged animal manure purchased in a bag from the garden center. Plants love sand in the root zone, so throw in a bit if it's on hand. It's best not to use soil dug from the garden because of the fungus spores and insect larvae likely included. You won't like what they'll get up to in your pot.

Environmental stress often causes plants in pots to deteriorate. Prolonged exposure to hot sun heats up the soil mass and can cook the roots. Constant wind causes foliage to transpire excessive amounts of moisture, dehydrating leaf tissues and causing them to wilt. Plants allowed to wilt repeatedly will suffer permanent damage. Cluster containers so they can make a micro-climate of cool air and humidity. Be sure they have shade for some part of the day, and protection from wind.

At the end of the season remove and discard the plants. If you want to transfer an outdoor container to indoors for the winter you must bring it in before there is a significant cooling of night temperatures, about the end of August in the north. If you wait until nights are chilled, the change in temperature indoors will cause defoliation. As well, be prepared for surprises. Some kind of insect life likely has found its way into the pot, and you may have to deal with a proliferation of wild stock. If you have a favorite plant and don't want to lose it, take cuttings and root them in mid-summer. You can grow them during winter as houseplants and take them outside next season.

Soil mix in the pots may be dumped on garden beds, where it will be a welcome organic amendment. Don't attempt to reuse it next year and risk fungus infections. Brush the containers out thoroughly and store them stacked upside-down in a basement or garage, or even under a deck. Clay pots can be kept outside if they are completely empty of soil and upside-down. If they are left outside containing soil, frost will cause the soil to expand and crack them.

A curved and winding path causes the eye to slow down and examine diversions along the way, prolonging interest and involving the viewer more thoughtfully in the garden. Straight paths send the viewer's gaze quickly to the back wall, shutting off possible avenues of discovery. But setting an object at the top of the path, like this black iron post, gives the eye a place to pause and consider the perennial beds on either side. In a more rustic setting, a large boulder could serve the same purpose.

Two

Garden ecology

Making the most of the site

Plants are not much different from people. They consume basic food products that they convert into energy. They breathe oxygen and drink water, require clean living conditions with sufficient light and are vulnerable to infection from viruses, bacteria and fungi. They respond vigorously to intelligent care, and suffer visibly from neglect and abuse. Plants do not whine but will dramatically demonstrate their distress about inadequate circumstances. Poor plant performance most often can be traced to deficiencies in one or all of the four basic health requirements: good soil structure, moisture, nutrients and light.

Knowing your garden's ecological profile at the start of a project can make the difference between time and money well spent and a dismal garden in decline. Deciding what site changes can be achieved within one growing season without a bank loan or advanced engineering skills will help you to order priorities. Simple site alterations can be of great benefit to any garden plan. Soil in a chronically dry site can be amended with organic materials to improve plant health, fertility and moisture retention. Drainage can be improved in a wet site by digging in builder's sand or installing weeping tiles. Soil with poor fertility can be enriched with compost, manure and organic fertilizers like blood meal, bone meal and kelp meal. A site with dense shade can be bright-ened by judicial high-pruning of dominant trees, or dappled shade can be created to cool a hot, dry area.

This is the moment when many irresistible gardening urges meet with the immovable force of site restrictions. Soil, moisture and light can be improved to a reasonable extent, but a complete change of the ecological environment is often not worthwhile or even achievable. Indulging a desire for luxuriant ferns and moisture-loving rhododendrons on a sunny hillside with gravelly soil and sharp drainage can only come to disappointment, even with intensive efforts to amend the soil. Far better to assess the bright and dry conditions and plant drought-resistant plants like sedum, perennial cranesbill geranium, artemisia and ornamental grasses. Similarly, a garden with areas of significantly poor drainage may be most successfully established with moisture-loving bog plants such as primula, marsh marigold (*Caltha palustris*, zone 2), ligularia and great lobelia (*Lobelia siphilitica*, zone 4). Happy is the gardener who plays the hand that's dealt.

*Previous page: Dry soils require plants that can adapt to arid circumstances. In character with the ecology of this site, the dry stream bed is planted with drought-hardy shrubs and perennials. Corkscrew hazel (*Corylus avellana 'Contorta', *zone 4) and smokebush (*Cotinus coggygria, *zone 4) are deciduous shrubs that will grow in dry conditions. Japanese garden juniper (*Juniperus procumbens 'Nana', zone 2) *and 'Turquoise Spreader' juniper (*J. horizontalis, *zone 3) provide texture as they spread across the rocks. Dwarf red pines (*Pinus resinosa, *zone 2) are strong vertical features, and tall grasses and creeping hens and chickens (*Sempervivum spp.) *give detail to this dry garden.*

Soil

Beneath our feet

City soil is full of history. Dig it, and you may unearth relics from the last occupants or previous civilizations. Soil is a repository for buried treasures, buried garbage, buried secrets. It makes good sense to know as much as possible about the history of your garden soil, as this may hold the answers to questions down the road. Local historical societies, libraries and municipal boards may have old records of development on the site, and even neighbors may remember events going back several decades.

Soil in older residential neighborhoods is not likely to harbor unpleasant surprises. If the site has been a garden or lawn for fifty years or longer, there is usually an 8 to 10-inch (20 to 23 cm) layer of topsoil in place and no garbage or chemical spills underneath. New houses, however, may have very shallow topsoil, as little as 2 inches (5 cm), and a fair amount of construction debris buried under the lawn. Mushrooms sprouting up in this

Causes for poor plant performance

Compacted soil with poor drainage and low oxygen

Compacted soil lacks oxygen and adequate water drainage.

Moss and fungus grow on the soil surface and infect plants in wet seasons.

Plants show poor vigor and little new growth in spring.

Stems and branches don't lengthen.

Low bud and flower production; many buds fail to develop and fall off.

Plant life is shortened, branches begin to die, steady decline each season.

Lack of moisture

Insufficient moisture interrupts root growth and stem and flower production.

Plant growth slows abruptly after early spring.

Plant development is stunted by mid-summer.

Plants wilt dramatically at mid-day.

Few flower buds are formed.

Flower buds fail to develop and fall off.

Leaves have crisp brown edges.

Leaf centers appear scorched.

Foliage begins to drop off in late summer.

Stems are thin and brittle.

Few seeds are formed.

Poor nutrients

Plants lack elements necessary for growth and health.

Pale or yellow leaf color.

Weak, floppy stems.

Plants fail to reach normal height.

Poor flowering and fruiting.

Stunted root growth.

Purple flush to underside of leaves.

Reduced disease resistance.

Blossom-end rot in tomatoes.

Low light

Plants suffer from poor vigor and low energy.

Delayed growth in spring.

Small leaves.

Few flowers and fruit.

Tall, lanky growth.

Shrubs are thin and spindly.

Perennial clumps don't increase.

lawn are indicators of the wood buried below, and intensive efforts may be necessary to develop growable soil. Housing built on what was once farmland or golf courses may have pesticide residues in the soil. And gardens in former industrial areas can have deposits of lead and other heavy metals. Almost everything can be dealt with in one way or another, but it's a good idea to get a detailed soil analysis and know what you've got.

Soil that has simply been neglected can be improved and made fertile with the addition of organic materials like compost, leaves and aged manure. Metal and industrial chemical pollutants can remain permanently in the soil. Replacing the soil is sometimes the only solution. Pesticides will degrade over time, but this can be a long, slow process. If your soil is seriously laden with any kind of pollutant, contact the city health department. It's likely other garden owners in your area have the same problem and assistance may be readily available.

About compost

The very best food for plants can't be bought for any price. Compost is homemade humus, the product of ornamental and vegetable plant parts that have been decomposed by natural soil microbes. Many forms of compost can be bought in garden centers, but the best way to know what you've got is to make it yourself. Any pile of organic material will slowly rot and return its minerals to the soil, but the process is sped along by cutting the stems and leaves in small pieces and turning the pile to incorporate oxygen. Feel the pile with your hand each time something is added. The materials should be sponge-damp. Add a sprinkling of water if necessary. Turn or ruffle the pile with a garden fork every three or four weeks. Compost is most efficiently made by mixing fresh green and dead brown ingredients in a ratio of 4 to 1. The green materials are garden refuse and kitchen vegetable trimmings (no meat, bones, fats or dairy products). The brown material is dead leaves collected in autumn and saved in plastic bags. (Keep the bags open to prevent the ammonia smell produced by decomposition with low oxygen.) After a year the compost will be dark brown

Harvesting humus

Leaf mold is a good source of freshly made humus, the fibrous product of decomposing organic materials. In a forest, humus is the layer of brown crumbly material lying under the fallen leaf litter that is not yet decomposed.

To make your own supply of leaf mold, choose a small area of your garden for permanent production. Each autumn, pile leaves 3 feet (90 cm) deep and mix in a generous amount of composted animal manure, turning the pile roughly with a fork to mix and aerate. Cover loosely with a large sheet of plastic weighted down at the corners with bricks or stones, leaving open spaces along the edges for ventilation. After the last expected snowfall, remove the plastic covering. In June repeat the rough turning. By October most of the leaves will be decomposed into leaf mold, and the humus is ready to be spread on beds and over the roots of shrubs and trees.

Locating the bin near the source of raw materials helps to ensure a maximum amount of finished compost. Making compost is fun when the process is convenient and accessible to the gardener, but less inviting a task when plant debris must be hauled any distance. The spent flowers of chives and stalks of dill will be cut down and put right into the bin discreetly in the corner. Composting is a good and honorable gardening endeavor, and there's nothing wrong with placing the bin in a centrally visible spot, surrounded with plants that grow to enormous proportions, feeding off the riches within.

and crumbly, ready to be spread on growing beds and in planting holes.

You can boost the nutritional content of your finished compost by adding coffee grounds (nitrogen), egg shells (calcium) and banana peels (potassium). Watering the compost pile periodically with kelp seaweed extract will enhance the fertility of the finished product with micro-nutrients and plant growth hormones.

Making the soil efficient

A healthy soil is a system with great capabilities. It readily accepts moisture from rain or irrigation and allows it to percolate downward through tiny spaces, called pores, between clumps of soil and sand. Despite this efficient drainage action, the spongy web of organic material retains sufficient moisture in the root zone to hydrate plants. As excess moisture drains away, oxygen and nitrogen enter the

Testing for soil compaction

Choose an undisturbed area that has not been dug for plants, or a section of lawn. Lift a flap of turf grass by using a blunt-nosed spade to cut three sides of a one-foot (30 cm) square. Slide the spade under the flap of turf and lay it back to expose the soil.

Dig a hole approximately 10 inches (23 cm) deep, reserving the soil in a container, and flood the hole with water. Allow it to drain, then flood it again. If the second filling of water drains within two hours, soil pores are functioning well and exchanging adequate amounts of air and water.

pores to be absorbed by roots. Because plants do most of their eating, drinking and breathing underground, this continuous exchange of moisture and gases is the central factor in a healthy soil.

Soil with adequate space between soil clumps and efficient movement of water and gases has good physical structure, and is described as being in good tilth. The desirable ratio of ingredients in healthy soil is 40 percent stone minerals, 10 percent organic materials, 25 percent water and 25 percent air. Increasing the amount of organic material can make this good ratio even better.

You can send soil samples to testing services for constituent analysis, but most gardeners can figure out their soil's ratio for themselves. Healthy soil has its own fragrance, as satisfying and exciting as any rose. It is a subtle sweet and musky organic scent of natural elements in harmony. Some people liken it to the yeasty aroma of freshly baked bread. Like any good perfume, its primary elements can be separated. Soil in good tilth has the scent of moisture, clay, organic fibers in varying states of decomposition and also the freshness of air. The perfume is encountered up close when you're planting or when you're simply walking across the earth. Soil should not have any sour, rank or fetid odors.

Soil with good structure has its own distinguishable texture and feel. Take a handful and roll it between your fingers and thumb. The softness of soil in good tilth comes from the fine particles of silt and clay, each of their molecules lubricated and softened by an enveloping film of moisture. The slight grittiness of each sharp grain of sand is felt in contrast to the smooth mass. Bits of organic debris form the largest particles, with the mixed textures of irregular woody chunks, papery leaf bits and spongy fibers.

Gardeners can also judge the health and tilth of their soil by observing established plants. Good soil is reflected in strong plant vigor. Perennial plants demonstrate the strength of their growth with rapidly expand ing clump sizes and increasing numbers of flower buds. These are sure signs that root growth is taking place and that the soil is providing all the necessary elements to fuel the productive expansion. Woody shrubs show their growth by extending their canes higher and wider, sending up new canes from the base of the plant and breaking buds to create branching from the main canes. Trees grow in a similar manner, by rapidly extending central limbs, breaking buds to form branches and thickening their trunks.

Staying alive

No soil is ever really perfect, but coming close to perfection is not hard to do by monitoring the changing needs of your garden earth. A living soil with a healthy balance of minerals, humus, water and gases is kept alive by the annual renewal of organic materials. If trees still covered the earth, organic material would be automatically deposited on the garden in a perfect cycle of renewal. But that is generally not allowed to happen in city gardens, where

Closely watched weeds

Weeds have preferences for various kinds of soil and moisture conditions, and where they appear and grow vigorously is an indication of soil characteristics.

Sandy soil, loose texture, low moisture

Field bindweed, *Convolvulus arvensis*
Field horsetail, *Equisetum arvense*
Sheep sorrel, *Rumex acetosella*

Dense clay, excessively wet, poor drainage

Canada thistle, *Cirsium arvense*
Creeping buttercup, *Ranunculus repens*
Ox-eye daisy, *Chrysanthemum leucanthemum*

Heavy clay, hard texture, tending to dryness.

Dandelion, *Taraxacum officinale*
Plaintains, *Plantago* spp.
Quack grass, *Agropyron repens*

Clay-loam, heavy texture, sufficient humus and moisture

Chickweed, *Stellaria media*
Chicory, *Cichorium intybus*
Redroot pigweed, *Amaranthus retroflexus*

The fertility of soil in good tilth produces impressive growth and flowering. Roses are heavy feeders and require substantial amounts of oxygen and consistent moisture in the root zone. The explosion of growth in this tiny urban rose garden reflects the care lavished on soil preparation. No amount of fertilizer can compensate for poor soil structure. But generous additions of compost, aged manure and sharp sand will encourage the growth of bionic roses.

leaves may be considered messy and quickly bagged for refuse collection. Yet soil requires a continuous replenishment of organic material to maintain efficient structure and fertility.

Renewing organic material is a task that becomes a gardening enthusiasm once you see the response in plant growth. Soil animals and microbes have big appetites for decaying bits of dead organisms. These efficient decomposers need a fresh supply of fibrous organic material to continue producing the humus so essential to soil fertility and prospering plants.

Organizing the feeding of soil life is fairly simple. A soil with adequate tilth and structure doesn't need to have organic material dug in. In fact, unnecessary tilling does more harm than good, upsetting the layers of soil organisms and generally disrupting the pore system for a time. Organic materials laid on the soil

Almost-instant soil

Soil production through normal geologic methods requires about six thousand years. But in a pinch, good organic soil can be manufactured in six months.

In autumn, when quantities of tree leaves are available, mix 3 parts shredded tree leaves with 1 part sharp builder's sand and 1 part composted animal manure. This rough mix can be made in any volume and placed where you intend to plant next spring. Over the winter the mix will sink down and begin to degrade into a rough texture that you can plant in by spring. By the end of the growing season it will have the finer texture of aged soil.

surface are accessible to worms and smaller organisms, and they will come up to get it. Smaller pieces of leaf and stem debris have more exposed surfaces for quick consumption and will disappear into the soil more rapidly than larger pieces.

Organic materials like compost and manure can be spread over the soil surface at any time to suit the gardener's schedule. Shredded bark purchased in large bags, pine needles and fresh, unsprayed grass clippings from the lawn can be supplied in one big amount, or in several smaller applications when these materials become available. The choice of organic materials should be guided by practicality and availability, and if they are laid down as a mulch, they must also be aesthetically pleasing. Strange choices like old cotton clothing and shredded mattresses are organic materials that will feed the soil, but no one wants to look at them in the garden.

Compost piles produce the best soil amendment of any kind, but not every garden can accommodate composting. Smaller gardens often have difficulty housing the plastic bins. Composting kitchen and garden debris in bins is an efficient method of waste management, but it produces limited amounts of finished compost. Even that small amount is worthwhile, though, and can be reserved for use on favorite plants. Producing larger amounts to spread throughout the garden requires a much bigger compost pile, one many gardeners don't have room for. Municipally produced leaf compost is often available free for the labor of bagging it, but sometimes the quality is inconsistent and it may be necessary to screen or rake out branches and chunks of wood.

Freshly fallen leaves are generously available in autumn and can be laid on plant beds and along the base of hedges and shrubs as an

Buying in bulk

When ordering large quantities of soil amendments, it can be difficult to estimate the amount required. Nurseries, building centers and soil companies will want to know your needs in measurements of cubic yards. Many garden products are sold this way: topsoil, triple mix, composted manure, sand, grit, gravel, shredded bark, bark chips and brick chips.

First, measure the soil areas you intend to improve, noting the length and width in feet. Irregular shapes can be roughly estimated. Deciding how many inches in depth are required of the amendments depends on the current condition of the soil. To make a reasonable improvement, you will need to spread 4 inches of manure and 2 inches of builder's sand over the soil and dig it in. Double the amounts for soil in very poor condition. Use this formula to calculate the quantity you will need to order in cubic yards:

Length (in feet) x width (in feet) x depth (in inches) ÷ 324 = cubic yards

(Length (in meters) x width (in meters) x depth (in centimeters) ÷ 100 = cubic meters)

Example: You have a planting bed with compacted soil, measuring approximately 14 feet (4.3 m) in length and 10 feet (3 m) in depth. You want to dig in 6 inches (15 cm) of sharp builder's sand. How much sand should you order?

14 x 10 x 6 = 840 ÷ 324 = 2.59 cubic yards

(4.3 x 3 x 15 = 193.5 ÷ 100 = 1.94 cubic meters)

Be generous with the sand and order 3 cubic yards (2 cubic meters). The plants will love it!

annual organic amendment. Putting the leaves through a shredder or mulching mower insures they will stay in place and not be carried away by wind, and also makes a very attractive and sweet-smelling surface covering. Small leaves like apple, birch, locust, silver maple and serviceberry can be used whole without shredding, but broad leaves like Norway maple and oak need to be reduced in size to prevent matting.

Leaves put down in autumn should be 2 to 3 inches (5 to 7.5 cm) deep, and will rapidly sink when wet. This is a permanent form of mulch and should remain in place until it is consumed by the soil in approximately a year, and then it's time to do it again. Lawns can be continually mulched by leaving the clippings in place, and plant debris gathered from perennial beds can be finely chopped and then spread over the soil surface.

Pine needles are an excellent organic material to combine with soil. Their resin makes them high in acid, but it is released very slowly and doesn't have a significant effect on pH, the measurement of soil acidity and alkalinity. Their greatest benefit is an ability to aerate the soil. The needles don't lie completely flat, and their slight curvature retains tiny pockets of air about them, which is very beneficial to plant roots.

Some nitrogen-fixing plants for city gardens

Shrubs, trees and vines

Cutleaf peashrub (shrub), *Caragana arborescens* 'Lobergii', zone 2, 8 feet (2.4 m)
Golden chain tree, *Laburnum* x *watereri* 'Vossii', zone 5, 9 feet (2.7 m)
Imperial honeylocust, *Gleditsia triacanthos* var. *inermis*, zone 4, 30 feet (9 m)
Japanese wisteria (vine), *Wisteria floribunda*, zone 4, up to 30 feet (9 m)
Katsura tree, *Cercidiphyllum japonicum*, zone 4, 30 feet (9 m)
Kentucky coffee tree, *Gymnocladus dioicus*, zone 4, 40 feet (12 m)
Lablab bean (annual vine), *Dolichos lablab*, zone 5, 10 feet (3 m)
Mimosa, *Albizia julibrissin* 'E.H. Wilson' ('Rosea'), zone 6, 20 feet (6 m)

Morning glory (annual vine), *Convolvulus* hybrids, zone 5, 10 feet (3 m)
Perennial pea vine, *Lathyrus latifolius*, zone 3, 9 feet (2.7 m)
Redbud, *Cercis canadensis*, zone 5, 25 feet (7.5 m)
Umbrella tree, *Catalpa bungei*, zone 5, 12 feet (3.5 m)

Perennials

False indigo, *Baptisia australis*, zone 3, 36 inches (90 cm)
Goat's rue, *Galega officinalis*, zone 3, 36 inches (90 cm)
Lupin, *Lupinus* spp., zone 4, 18 to 36 inches (90 cm)
Mountain thermopsis, *Thermopsis montana*, zone 3, 24 inches (60 cm)
Purple clover, *Trifolium repens* 'Atropurpureum', zone 3, 3 inches (7.5 cm)
Spring vetchling, *Lathyrus vernus*, zone 4, 12 to 15 inches (30 to 38 cm)

The gardener's companion

Worms are what we want. Their ability to mix, dig, burrow and fertilize soil is prodigious, and they are unfailing indicators of good tilth and fertility. Their favorite diet is decomposing brown leaf tissue, although they will turn any organic debris into humus and fertilizer. In their burrowing and earth-turning maneuvers, worms carry organic material and air down and bring mineral nutrients to the surface. They are able to dig through heavy clay and shift stone particles fifty times their own weight, tasks gardeners prefer not to contemplate.

Worm castings are an ideal form of animal manure and contain 50 percent organic matter plus eleven trace minerals. A thriving worm colony is the garden's greatest resource, and should be protected from pesticides and manufactured fertilizers, which will seriously decrease their numbers. Healthy soil should have five to seven worms per square foot, and this is easily monitored by counting the worms in two spadefuls of earth. To get more worms and encourage the growth of the colony, use shredded leaf mulch on the surface of planting beds and allow fallen leaves to remain under shrubs and trees. Moderate amounts of fallen leaves lying on lawns in autumn can be shredded by a power mower; just leave the chopped pieces on the lawn.

What's all this about pH?

Much rewarding gardening takes place using trial-and-error methods. Yet a simple understanding of the basic chemical character of soil can save time and frustration when things inexplicably go wrong. Soil chemistry is not mysterious, but it is complex, and it's awe-inspiring to learn about the powerful interaction of chemical elements going on underground. With all that activity, surely there should be more noise.

Every soil has a level of acidity and alkalinity that can be measured on the pH scale, running from 0 to 14. The scale is an indication of the concentration of hydrogen ions that are associated with available soil fertility

Apples don't love devil's food

The acidity or alkalinity of soil and almost anything organic can be measured by preparing a slurry of the substance with de-ionized water and testing it with a pH probe and meter. And the results are sometimes surprising.

Limes	1.8	Bread	5.3
Ginger ale	2.0	Brussels sprouts	6.0
McIntosh apples	3.3	Cocoa	6.3
Mayonnaise	4.2	Chicken	6.5
Eclairs	4.4	Crabs	7.0
Buttermilk	4.5	Camembert	7.4
Ground beef	5.1	Devil's food cake	7.5
Turnips	5.2		

(pH means parts hydrogen). The middle point, pH 7.0, is a neutral level. Values below 7.0 are acidic, and values above the neutral point are alkaline.

The ideal point for most plant growth is between pH 6.3 and pH 6.8, or a slightly acid reading of a soil sample. At this level, nutrients are freely available, soil animals and biological life are most active and fertility is high. Most plants have difficulty absorbing nutrients when the soil is either strongly acidic (below pH 5.0) or strongly alkaline (above pH 8.0). Exceptions are ericacious plants, which perform best in acidic soil of about pH 5.5 or lower. This group includes rhododendron, azalea, pieris, enkianthus, leucothoe and heather.

The factors endowing a soil with its acid or alkaline character are large and generally unchangeable. Bedrock buried deep under the soil has a dominating role in establishing pH

*A freshly made bed is kept weed free with a 3-inch blanket of shredded-bark mulch that prevents light from reaching weed seeds. The mulch reduces evaporation of soil moisture by sun and wind, protects topsoil from erosion and will eventually degrade in place and improve soil fertility. The dramatically weeping false cypress (*Chamaecyparis nootkatensis *'Pendula', zone 5) is a useful specimen plant with enough character to stand alone and direct traffic along the driveway.*

and keeping it at a consistent level. Gardens over limestone bedrock will have alkaline soil; gardens over granite bedrock are more likely to have acidic soil. Moisture also has an influence: dry soil tends toward alkalinity, and wet soils are more acidic.

Additions of limestone or sulfur, both organic elements, can moderate pH. Adding calcitic or dolomitic limestone raises the pH of an acidic soil to a more acceptable level, whereas sulfur lowers the pH of a strongly alkaline soil. But these manipulations are effective for a very short time, perhaps less than one growing season, and the soil quickly returns to its true pH value.

Organic plant material is the only soil constituent with any significant and lasting effect on pH. Humus has an ability to buffer acidity and alkalinity, and its presence in quantity is directly commensurate with the ability of plants to adapt to soil pH outside their ideal range. While it is useful to have your soil pH determined by a local or regional testing service, the most effective thing gardeners can do to achieve the best soil possible is to add generous amounts of organic mulch materials each year. So keep on trucking.

Compacted clay, worst-case scenario

Clay has no shortage of critics with sore backs. It's well to remember that the minerals found in clay particles are essential plant foods and

A group of containers outside the author's kitchen is a quick-fix garden when there isn't time to get down the steps into the real thing. Old baskets, fiberboard pots, plastic bins and terra cotta hold a collection of tender annuals, herbs, vegetables and strawberries. The mean-looking stone bunny keeps marauding raccoons at bay. Plants are discarded in late autumn and the premium soil mix (2 parts aged manure, 1 part peat moss, 1 part sharp sand) is emptied into garden beds where improvement is needed.

contribute to fertility. Clay is useful and necessary, but it must be offered to plants in careful balance with organic materials and in a soil of proper structure. Sad but true, when clay is dense and compacted, with little oxygen content, it's bad news.

Compacted clay has little humus content, resulting in fewer and smaller pore spaces that hold water tightly between tiny crumbs of soil and drain slowly. Extremely compacted soils can be difficult to wet, but once water is forced into them, they can be almost impossible to drain. Very little air and minimal organic material are able to enter heavy clay soil, and it is likely to be deficient in oxygen, nitrogen, worms and other biological life. The primary characteristic of wet clay is a dense and sticky texture into which tender plant roots cannot successfully penetrate. Plants growing in compacted wet clay often decline miserably over time from oxygen deprivation. In its worst form, wet clay soil can be effectively dead, lacking the necessities of life for soil organisms and plants.

In excessively dry conditions, clay soil may harden and shrink, opening wide cracks in the earth and preventing moisture from entering the hardened surface. Dry compacted soil is often the reason some lawns suffer chronically from drought. Wetting a soil in this condition is difficult, as the hardened clay initially sheds water until the surface is softened. The absence of an effective pore system to carry water down through the root zone causes moisture to accumulate in the top few inches of the surface soil. Plants in dry clay soils develop shallow root systems that are vulnerable to high soil temperatures, and their growth potential is significantly limited.

Most clay soils found in urban gardens are not this extreme, but they can be difficult to grapple with at first. Plants will suffer from oxygen deprivation and poor energy production. They will grow slowly, or perhaps not at all. The high energy requirements of flowers and fruits may result in little ornamental production, and root systems unable to penetrate the soil will be abbreviated and sparse. This condition is sometimes found where clay soil is excessively irrigated by in-ground automatic sprinkler systems and plants are in obvious decline.

Restoring compacted clay soils

The good news is that most clay soils, wet or dry, can be altered and brought to a state of adequate function. Restoring the balance will take many seasons, but encouraging results can be had almost immediately.

The first step is to loosen the clay particles so that necessary amendments can be introduced. The most effective way to do this is to spread at least 3 inches of sharp builder's sand and pea gravel over the soil and dig it in. Use a stiff rake to break up clods and grade the earth.

Organic materials are also a crucial amendment. They can be spread on top of the sand

Plants that tolerate wet soil

Perennials

Astilbe, *Astilbe* spp., zone 4,8 to 30 inches (20 to 75 cm)
Bee balm, *Monarda didy*ma, zone 4, 48 inches (120 cm)
Bigleaf ligularia, *Ligularia dentata*, zone 4, 36 inches (90 cm)
Cardinal flower, *Lobelia cardinalis*, zone 3, 36 inches (90 cm)
Creeping jenny, *Lysimachia nummularia*, zone 3, 3 inches (7.5 cm)
Culver's root, *Veronicastrum virginicum*, zone 3, 60 inches (150 cm)
Fingerleaf rodgersia, *Rodgersia aesculifolia*, zone 5, 36 inches (90 cm)
Japanese iris, *Iris ensata*, zone 5, 36 inches (90 cm)
Japanese primula, *Primula japonica*, zone 5, 18 inches (45 cm)
Joe-pye weed, *Eupatorium maculatum*, zone 5, 72 inches (180 cm)
Marsh marigold, *Caltha palustris*, zone 3,10 inches (23 cm)
Meadow rue, *Thalictrum* spp., zone 4, 24 to 60 inches (60 to 150 cm)
Monkshood, *Aconitum* spp., zone 3, 24 to 72 inches (60 to 180 cm)
New England aster, *Aster novae-angliae*, zone 3, 48 inches (120 cm)
Ornamental rhubarb, *Rheum palmatum*, zone 4, 60 inches (150 cm)
Purple loosestrife, *Lythrum salicaria*, (except in wetlands), zone 3, 48 inches (120 cm)
Queen-of-the-meadow, *Filipendula ulmaria*, zone 3, 48 inches (120 cm)
Queen-of-the-prairie, *Filipendula rubra*, zone 3, 60 inches (150 cm)
Siberian bugloss, *Brunnera macrophylla*, zone 3, 24 inches (60 cm)
Siberian iris, *Iris sibirica*, zone 4, 36 inches (90 cm)
Spiderwort, *Tradescantia obiensis*, zone 5, 36 inches (90 cm)
Turtlehead, *Chelone barbatus*, zone 4, 36 inches (90 cm)

Shrubs

American elder, *Sambucus canadensis*, zone 4, 5 to 12 feet (1.5 to 3.5 m)
American holly, *Ilex opaca*, zone 5, 40 to 50 feet (12 to 15 m)
American snowbell, *Styrax americanus*, zone 5, 6 to 8 feet (1.8 to 2.4 m)
Chokeberry, *Aronia* spp, zone 4, 6 to 10 feet (1.8 to 3 m)
Finetooth holly hybrids, *Ilex serrata* x *I. verticillata*, zone 5, 10 to 15 feet (3 to 4.5 m)
Purple osier willow, *Salix purpurea*, zone 3, 8 to 10 feet (2.4 to 3 m)
Pussy willow, *Salix caprea*, zone 4, 15 to 25 feet (4.5 to 7.5 m)
Silverleaf dogwood, *Cornus alba* 'Elegantissima', zone 2, 6 to 10 feet (1.8 to 3 m)
Summersweet clethra, *Clethra alnifolia*, zone 4, 3 to 8 feet (90 to 240 cm)
Virginia sweetspire, *Itea virginica*, zone 5, 3 to 5 feet (90 to 150 cm)

Trees

American hornbeam, *Carpinus caroliniana*, zone 3, 20 to 30 feet (6 to 9 m)
Boxelder hybrids, *Acer negundo*, zone 2, 30 to 50 feet (9 to 15 m)
Honeylocust, *Gleditsia triacanthos* var. *inermis*, zone 4, 30 to 70 feet (9 to 21 m)
Pin oak, *Quercus palustris*, zone 4, 60 to 70 feet (18 to 21 m)
Red maple, *Acer rubrum*, zone 3, 40 to 60 feet (12 to 18 m)
River birch, *Betula nigra*, zone 4, 40 to 70 feet (12 to 21 m)
Silver poplar, *Populus alba*, zone 3, 40 to 60 feet (12 to 18 m)
Sweetbay magnolia, *Magnolia virginiana*, zone 5, 20 to 60 feet (6 to 18 m)
Sweetgum, *Liquidambar styraciflua*, zone 5, 60 to 70 feet (18 to 21 m)
Tamarack, *Larix laricina*, zone 1, 30 to 50 feet (9 to 15 m)
Tulip tree, *Liriodendron tulipifera*, zone 4, 70 to 90 feet (21 to 27.5 m)
Weeping willow, *Salix alba*, zone 4, 50 to 70 feet (15 to 21 m)

and dug in with it. Fallen tree leaves and any kind of pine or spruce needles are the most ideal materials for this purpose. Peat moss could also be combined into the mix if the budget allows. Shredded newspaper is another suitable amendment, but avoid any colored sheets. The inks contain undesirable chemicals derived from heavy metals.

The initial addition of sharp sand, pea gravel and organic materials should result in a rough but looser soil with improved ability to conduct water and air throughout the root zone. When accomplished with generous use of amendments and obsessive effort, this first big dig should be the only one necessary. Thereafter, apply thick layers of organic materials to the surface as a mulch to keep worms and microbes busy building new and better soil structure. As well, include generous amounts of sand and peat moss into the hole when you're adding new plants.

Clay-busting materials

ABOUT PEAT MOSS

Over many thousands of years, mossy plant material in boggy areas decays slowly in water with little oxygen present. Eventually a thick mass of fibrous humus is left to be harvested for horticultural purposes. The top layer is removed and sold as peat moss. When the current peat bogs are exhausted, that will be the end of this resource for many thousands of years. Harvesting also seriously endangers animals dependent on the ecology of the bogs.

The sphagnum peat moss sold in bales is an excellent source of organic material for the soil. It has no mineral nutrients or food value for plants but is a valuable soil conditioner, creating a spongy, moist soil environment. It is an acidic material, approximately pH 4, and of great benefit to acid-loving plants like rhododendrons and azaleas.

Peat moss should never be allowed to dry out, but unfortunately improper storage of bales often causes this to happen. When peat is too dry, it will shed water and be very difficult to wet. If put into the earth in this condition, it will remain underground in a dry state and be of little value to soil and plants. When opening a bale, if the peat feels dry and dusty, place it in a wheelbarrow or on a tarp, add hot water (dry peat moss will not absorb cold water) and mix thoroughly.

The peat moss sold in bales has a very fine, dustlike consistency that degrades rapidly in the earth. While it's an excellent soil conditioner, its rapid decomposition makes a poor value for money. Leaves are an excellent substitute, with nutritive benefit to plants and much longer action in soil, although they do not have a comparable acid content.

ABOUT SAND AND GRAVEL

Sand and gravel are useful additions to soil, breaking up masses of clay and creating spaces for air and water. But using the right particle size is important.

Sand used as a soil conditioner must be in the form of large, rough grains. Sharp sand, builder's sand and concrete sand are all basically the same size, and the individual grains can be felt when pinched between the fingers. Play sand for children's activities and sandboxes is too fine, without the sharp edges for breaking up clods. It will hold water instead of releasing it, compounding the problems of clay soil. Beach sand is variable in particle size, from fine to coarse, and may contain salt, bacteria and residue from water pollutants. Best not to use it.

Gravel used as a soil conditioner must have a small particle size, no more than half an inch. Fine gravel or pea gravel are both suitable sizes. Larger gravel sizes tend to separate out from the soil and rise to the surface.

For breaking up clay soils, use a ratio of 2 parts sharp sand and 1 part fine gravel.

Even with regular irrigation, perennial plants in south-facing flower beds can suffer heat stress and frequent wilts in intense sunlight. This bed has no shade at all, but plants have been carefully chosen for their ability to stand up and perform in hot locations. Crowded together are salvia, dianthus, campanula, coneflower, evening primrose, yarrow, phlox and lavatera — all low-maintenance perennials able to maintain rigid stems and bright colors in high heat.

Sandy soil: too much of a good thing

There is no doubt that plants love sand for its large particle size and the air this brings into the root zone. Sand added to a soil mix in containers or in the ground always encourages growth. Roots will grow aggressively through sand as long as it contains moisture. But overly sandy and gravelly soils can lack sufficient organic materials to hold adequate moisture in the root zone and small clay particles to provide molecules of mineral nutrients. Rain and irrigation drain from it rapidly, leaving the soil arid and infertile with little biological life. The chronic moisture shortage causes plants to suffer frequent wilting, poor energy production and loss of roots and branches. Large trees and shrubs in sandy soil can be overcome by a permanent wilt in seasonal heat and may lose their leaves prematurely in late summer. Plants generally fail to grow when deprived of both moisture and nutrients. It is a futile struggle to keep pouring water on an overly porous soil.

Solutions are obvious and at hand. Soils high in sand and gravel content need to have the organic stuff of life put back into them. Any amount of gardener's gold, homemade compost, is a valuable contribution for its humus content and as a source of living biological organisms. But because there is never enough compost, also add composted animal manures, leaves, shredded black-and-white newspaper and peat moss.

In sandy conditions some amount of purchased topsoil or triple mix is a useful amendment. Topsoil has a high clay content, and it makes little sense to add this to a soil where excess clay is already a problem. But sandy soils are short on clay and its nutrients, and purchased soil will help to build fertility and hold moisture near plant roots. Triple mix is an enriched soil, with additions of composted manure and peat moss. It costs more than topsoil, but is a good material for use in planting holes and should become a standard ingredient for installations of new plants. Organic amendments and soil need to be dug into sandy soil, but the labor is easier than in a clay soil.

Mulches are important to shade sandy soil, preventing evaporation of precious moisture and lowering the soil temperature. Grains of sand heat up when exposed to sunlight and burn plant roots, just as sand at a beach can burn your feet. Mulch beds and borders with 3 inches (7.5 cm) of organic material such as shredded leaves or bark. The smallest size of bark chips also functions well as a mulch, but larger chips degrade unevenly and take on an unnatural manufactured appearance.

Gardeners may feel they need to rely on manufactured fertilizers with high numbers to supplement the starvation diet for plants in porous soils. However, because water leaches rapidly through the sand and gravel, fertilizers can leave salt residues behind, to accumulate in

Plants that tolerate dry soil

Perennials

Calamint, *Calamintha grandiflora*, zone 5, 18 inches (45 cm)

Catmint, *Nepeta sibirica*, zone 3, 24 inches (60 cm)

Common thyme, *Thymus vulgaris*, zone 5, 8 inches (20 cm)

Donkeytail spurge, *Euphorbia myrsinites*, zone 5, 8 inches (20 cm)

Globe thistle, *Echinops ritro*, zone 3, 36 inches (90 cm)

Golden feverfew, *Chrysanthemum parthenium*, zone 4, 12 inches (30 cm)

Houseleek, *Sempervivum* hybrids, zone 5, 6 inches (15 cm)

Lamb's-ears betony, *Stachys byzantina*, zone 4, 18 inches (45 cm)

Mugwort, *Artemisia* spp., zone 4, 12 inches (30 cm)

Ornamental sage, *Salvia* x *superba*, zone 5, 24 inches (60 cm)

Purple coneflower, *Echinacea purpurea*, zone 3, 36 inches (90 cm)

Stonecrop, *Sedum* hybrids, zone 4, 6 to 24 inches (60 cm)

Sundrops, *Oenothera tetragona*, zone 4, 24 inches (60 cm)

Shrubs

Autumn olive, *Elaeagnus umbellata*, zone 3, 8 to 12 feet (2.4 to 3.5 m)

Black jetbead, *Rhodotypos scandens*, zone 4, 3 to 6 feet (90 to 180 cm)

Cinquefoil, *Potentilla fruticosa*, zone 2, 3 to 4 feet (90 to 120 cm)

False spirea, *Sorbaria sorbifolia*, zone 3, 6 to 12 feet (1.8 to 3.5 m)

Fiveleaf aralia, *Acanthopanax sieboldianus*, zone 4, 5 to 10 feet (1.5 to 3 m)

Fragrant sumac, *Rhus aromatica*, zone 3, 6 to 10 feet (1.8 to 3 m)

Ninebark, *Physocarpus opulifolius*, zone 2, 5 to 10 feet (1.5 to 3 m)

Cotoneaster, *Cotoneaster* , zone 5, 2 to 3 feet (60 to 90 cm)

Rugosa rose, *Rosa rugosa*, zone 2, 4 to 6 feet (1.2 to 1.8 m)

Siberian peashrub, *Caragana arborescens*, zone 2, 10 to 20 feet (3 to 6 m)

Smokebush, *Cotinus coggygria*, zone 4, 10 to 15 feet (3 to 4.5 m)

Snowberry, *Symphoricarpos albus*, zone 3, 3 to 6 feet (90 to 180 cm)

Trees

Amur maple, *Acer ginnala*, zone 3, 12 to 18 feet (3.5 to 5.5 m)

Black locust, *Robinia pseudoacacia*, zone 3, 30 to 50 feet (9 to 15 m)

Chanticleer callery pear, *Pyrus calleryana* 'Chanticleer', zone 5, 25 to 35 feet (7.5 to 10.7 m)

Columnar English oak, *Quercus robur* 'Fastigiata', zone 3, 30 to 50 feet (9 to 15 m)

Devil's-walking stick, *Aralia spinosa*, zone 4, 10 to 20 feet (3 to 6 m)

European hornbeam, *Carpinus betulus*, zone 4, 40 to 60 feet (12 to 18 m)

Ginkgo, *Ginkgo biloba*, zone 4, 50 to 80 feet (15 to 24 m)

Goldenrain tree, *Koelreuteria paniculata*, zone 5, 30 to 40 feet (9 to 12 m)

Green ash, *Fraxinus pennsylvanica*, zone 3, 50 to 60 feet (15 to 18 m)

Hedge maple, *Acer campestre*, zone 4, 20 to 35 feet (6 to 10.7 m)

Japanese angelica tree, *Aralia elata*, zone 4, 20 to 30 feet (6 to 9 m)

Littleleaf linden, *Tilia cordata*, zone 3, 50 to 70 feet (15 to 21 cm)

Northern catalpa, *Catalpa speciosa*, zone 4, 20 to 40 feet (6 to 12 m)

Russian olive, *Elaeagnus angustifolia*, zone 2, 12 to 20 feet (3.5 to 6 m)

Stribling white mulberry, *Morus alba* 'Stribling', zone 4, 20 to 30 feet (6 to 9 m)

Tree-of-heaven, *Ailanthus altissima*, zone 4, 40 to 60 feet (12 to 18 m)

Trident maple, *Acer buergeranum*, zone 5, 20 to 30 feet (6 to 9 m) ever-increasing potency. Roots may be burned and plant growth stunted by this rich, salty diet. It's therefore far better to use organic fertilizers with lower numbers. When gardeners feed the soil a healthy diet, the soil has the best resources to feed the plants.

A combination of direct sun and sandy soil makes growing conditions harsh and challenging. A bit of partial shade, however, encourages better root growth and plant performance. Small groups, or copses, of shrubs can be installed to create areas of microclimate, providing cooler air and soil temperatures for perennial plants. Effective microclimates are structured by placing three to five small trees (under 15 feet (4.5 m) in height) in a triangular pattern, with massed perennials contained between them. Water is conserved by the lower soil temperature, and plants help each other out by shading the earth with their foliage.

Leguminous plants, like morning glories and lupins, which can be recognized by their pods containing bean-like seeds, are generally drought-hardy. They take gaseous nitrogen from air and convert it into solid granules, which feed themselves and other plants nearby. This is accomplished with the assistance of *Rhizobium* bacteria commonly found in garden soil and used by plant roots to convert nitrogen. Legumes always improve the fertility of porous soil. A powdered soil inoculant of friendly, clean *Rhizobium* is sold by garden centers and seed catalogues. Sprinkle some into the planting hole to increase flower production and soil fertility.

The addition of a simple trellis is the catalyst that makes this city doorstep into a small cottage garden. Shade from mature trees limits what can be grown, but elevating plants in containers increases the available light. Imperial Japanese morning glories and Old Spice sweet peas climb the trellis (in scale with its companion door), surrounded by a spontaneous cluster of chives, chrysanthemums, ivy and scented geraniums, tender fuchsia and the lime-green wands of annual helichrysum 'Limelight'. Despite the low light conditions, these plants put on a worthwhile display.

Three

Perennials, beds and borders

A bit of what you fancy

Few categories of gardening give so much pleasure or engender such anxiety as perennial plants. What is admired and reassuring about perennials is that, unlike annuals, they come back, usually bigger and better, each season. The initial investment in purchasing perennials is often cited as cost saving. And the fact that perennials also often require dividing means that more plants are achieved and the sense of investment grows.

Perennials are an avenue through which gardeners are able to get things exactly the way they want them, down to the finest specification of color, line and texture. The startling numbers of plants available and the deeply diverse gene pools they come from ensure that any nuance of gardening interest can be satisfied. The chartreuse blossoms of the lovely lady's mantle (*Alchemilla mollis*, zone 4) sway forward at a fifty-degree angle, while the same flowering stems on the virtually identical hybrid *A. mollis* 'Robusta' are held more firmly aloft, though still not entirely perpendicular. As always, the glory is in the details.

City gardeners working with smaller spaces will need a plan for managing the growth and expansion of perennial plantings. Taking advantage of every bit of space, removing the lawn and taking down a little-used garage are common tactics for expanding space. Eventually the garden is reasonably full, but a love of plants is a lifetime pursuit and the gardener's interest and enthusiasm are still in high gear. To pass up the acquisition of a coveted plant simply for presumed lack of space can indicate only poor inventory planning or lack of vision. There is always room for new plants; it only needs to be found. This wisdom is the principal philosophy of city growers who practice pack-and-cram gardening. Gardeners who love plants are directed by impulse and desire. Space and placement can always be negotiated with a bit of artful reorganization.

Management tactics must be direct and sometimes ruthless. Plants that have not adapted well to the available moisture and light should be culled each season. Any that are plagued by insects or disease should be removed. Perennials with strong growth can be frequently divided and the divisions shared with neighbors and at local plant sales. Renovating perennial beds every five years allows for soil improvement and lets you choose which plants are permanent treasures and which are less interesting and can be given away.

Previous page: Not all perennial borders are a narrow strip along the fence. The irregular shape of an island bed in the lawn can divide areas and organize open space. This suburban border is a dynamic collection of tender summer bulbs, ornamental grasses, perennials, shrubs and vines. The rough stepping stone path leads through the border to the sheltered area under the broad pergola hung with Japanese wisteria and golden hops (Humulus lupulus 'Aureus', zone 3). In late summer the border is bright with variegated hybrids of obedience plant and phlox, blue and red grasses, purple heuchera, scarlet crocosmia and striped canna foliage. Weeping larch and a tall standard rose provide strong vertical references.

Where to put things

a house can carry flowering vines, and window boxes can display plants in four seasons.

Traditional planting areas like foundation strips and narrow boundary beds are limiting and confined, but they can be widened and their shapes changed and expanded. New beds allow great license for placement and can be installed as islands in lawns or in disregarded boulevard strips. Walls of all kinds are useful for flowering vines, and more delicate vines can climb up the larger ones.

Cottage solutions

Among the basic tenets of English cottage gardening is the placement of plants pretty much wherever they fall. This haphazard charm is fostered by legions of self-sowing perennial plants that spread their progeny where the wind blows, and the cottager is presumably relaxed enough to find this a suitable method of placement.

City gardeners who adopt this laid-back attitude can consider planting perennials and annuals more expansively. The possibilities are many: doorstep plantings, pathway borders and arbor entrances from the street and between front and back gardens. Arbors can also be placed in planting beds for supporting vines and creepers of all kinds. Lawns can be planted with early-spring bulbs and ephemeral perennials. And crevices in cracked masonry and between paving stones can be seeded with sprawling perennial plants. Four sides of

Expanding borders

The gardening year begins in late autumn, when a full appreciation of the past season is at hand and gardeners are in a critical mood. Anything that has fallen short of expectation now looms large in the immediate perception: dahlias in an embarrassing flop from insufficient irrigation and total lack of stakes; hostas overwhelming the primulas at their feet; Japanese anemones, having finally taken hold, marching straight into the desperately nurtured toad lilies. And not to forget the alarming color liaison that has taken place between red daylilies and magenta cranesbill geraniums.

This is the season for planning, not only for how to do things better next year but also for ways to liberate more growing space to accommodate the plants not yet possessed. As you feel the pinch of tight borders, your attention may be unavoidably drawn to square footage covered by lawn. Certainly there are good reasons for preserving the greensward, but a bit of revision never went amiss when neatening up the edges. Extending the borders farther into lawn territory is a simple way of easing the close quarters of plants and creating new venues for expansion. Shrinking the lawn is a subtle way to grab a bit of space without disrupting the broad picture. Straight cutting the ragged and uneven edges of the lawn and then removing even more grass can be accomplished twice annually, spring and autumn. But the jig is up when your lawn begins to resemble a grass path through lush botanical borders. Simply admit guilt and press on.

Making new beds

At some point in every gardening life, push is likely to come to shove, and significantly more planting space must be developed. Careful organization speeds things along. First, choose a location with suitable light and moisture for your new plants. Choice is a luxury in city gardens where less square footage is available. It may be necessary to reverse the thinking and determine what plants can be grown in the space and conditions available. Sometimes success comes not from achieving what is desired but rather from what is discovered through working with the site. Where low-lying soil is constantly wet and slow draining, for example, plans can be altered to accommodate bog plants such as primula, ferns, ligular-

ia and Joe-Pye weed (*Eupatorium purpureum*, zone 3). Or the discovery of shallow sand deposits in shade is an opportunity to develop a bed of such drought-hardy plants as barrenwort (*Epimedium* spp., zone 4), perennial *Geranium macrorrhizum* (several color choices, zone 3), lady's mantle (*Alchemilla mollis*, zone 3) and sweet woodruff (*Galium odoratum*, zone 3).

Place the new bed where it can be enjoyed in as many seasons as possible, and even from indoors. The size is dictated not only by what area is available but also by how much new venue you can adequately maintain. It should be within reach of some form of irrigation and not too close to major tree roots. Beds can be placed to bring attention to a particular area, or to draw the garden visitor more deeply into planned settings. A series of free-floating island beds can be set as lures and inducements to carry interest deeper into areas of planned surprises, such as unexpected sitting areas and hidden water features.

Shape is a matter of some importance. The line of a planting bed is one of the strongest elements in the garden, and its perfection or inadequacy is apparent from all vantage points. If the line is graceless or illogical, it will be a persistent irritation. As in so many matters of aesthetic principle, the gardener's eye is always drawn to the blemish on the smooth surface of the work.

Beds that run along a fence or other border line are easier to deal with because there is only one line to fuss over, and the garden will

*Determining the line of a bed or path is the single most influencing factor in the symmetry of a garden. Curved lines ideally flow in a natural, relaxed arc without unexpected bulges or illogical turns. On a slight slope, the carefully curved line of a planting bed follows the grade downward and is, in turn, followed by a random pathway of flagstone. The generous swelling of the curve makes this small garden appear larger, and soil in the bed is mounded to form a gentle berm. A star magnolia (*Magnolia stellata, zone 4) is the central plant on highest ground, providing ornamental features through four seasons.*

Setting large boulders

Boulder-sized rocks weighing several hundreds of pounds can be purchased from stone yards and are large assets in every respect. Their shape and mineral character bring interest to a garden in every season and all weathers, and their dimension is exciting in smaller city gardens.

- First consider what mineral family is preferred. Granite boulders are rounded and may have streaks of white or pink quartz and shiny flecks of mica to catch the light. Armor rock is more angular, with shades of charcoal gray, black and cream. Limestone has a creamy lava-like appearance, often with deep pitting ideal for rockery pockets.

- Never attempt to lift a rock weighing more than 50 lb (22.5 kg). Arrange for it to be delivered and have a cushioned place for it to rest. If the boulder is lifted from the truck by crane it will have a controlled landing, but if it is tipped from the truck the impact can break asphalt, cement or brick. Old rubber tires, carpet remnants or a discarded mattress make good cushions. Some repair work will be necessary if it rests on lawn.

- Prepare the final resting place for the boulder by making a shallow excavation in the soil. When it's in place the rock should appear to emerge naturally from the earth, not look as if it fell off the back of a truck. Expect a quarter to a third of the boulder to be underground.

- If the boulder weighs up to 300 lb. (135 kg), it can be moved to its location in a heavy construction wheelbarrow. Tip the wheelbarrow down and use a steel wrecking bar or crowbar to lever and flip the rock into the bucket. Boulders can also be dragged on pieces of carpet, in plastic snow sleds with nylon rope pulls or even on heavy corrugated cardboard. They can be rolled for short distances over several sections of steel pipe, each 2 to 4 inches (5 to 10 cm) in diameter and about 3 feet (90 cm) long.

- It's best not to dump the boulder directly into the prepared depression, because that is the most difficult place to make adjustments. Set it next to the spot and consider which end is the top and what side should be facing front. If it is now right-side-up it can be pushed and shimmied into place; or if it is upside-down it can be rolled into position. If it is backwards, nudge and shift it around. A very heavy rock can be adjusted by forcing the pointed end of a pick-ax 2 to 3 inches (5 to 7.5 cm) under the rock and levering it into place.

- The boulder may make a better presentation if one end is slightly elevated. Use the pick-ax to lift one side a few inches while a helper uses a spade to force earth underneath. Pack soil into the gaps all around and give the boulder a companion planting like ferns or Solomon's seal (*Polygonatum biflorum*, zone 4), placed close enough so that foliage drapes against the rock.

always be at the side of the picture. Island beds bring the matter of shape into consideration. Those who are organically minded may be drawn to traditional outlines of kidneys, shamrocks and amoebas. Emblematic themes are sometimes expressed in beds shaped as stars, fans or teapots. Anything goes when shaping your own planting bed.

The old tradition of laying out the line of a new bed with a rubber garden hose is still the most satisfying method. Lay the hose in what seems like a good line, and then go off to other activities. Later, have another look at it and make some adjustments if need be. Looking at the line from a second-floor window is also a good perspective. Continue to fiddle a few times, then leave the hose in place overnight. Look again in the morning. If you are satisfied, the perfect line has been found. If not, be patient. Finding the best line can take as long as a week. All too often what is achieved in haste comes to be regretted at leisure. Never attempt to rush into a line; keep working with it and fine-tuning until it is absolutely right. A good line is a thing of pleasure and pride, and it is the greatest flattery to be complimented on the beauty of one's garden lines.

Goodbye to grass

If turf grass must be removed, you have a choice of method and tools. Digging up the turf, turning it over, chopping it up and allowing it to remain in the soil will result in the most dreaded consequences. Despite all the turning and chopping, a considerable amount of grass will resurrect itself, struggling upward into the new planting with genuinely vengeful energy. This is the way all grasses attempt to heal disturbed earth and protect the soil.

The most miserable approach is to take a short spade and begin digging it out in clumps. This time-and labor-intensive work is hard on the backs of young and old workers alike. For a small area, at least use a long-handled shovel that will relieve some of the strain and weight of the turf.

The best method to clear a larger area is to rent a sod cutter. The machine is gasoline powered and pushed along like a lawn mower. It slides a wide blade under the turf and cuts it into neat strips that can be rolled up and used for patching lawn in another place. Handling this machine requires fairly strong arms, but it makes quick and neat work of an unpleasant task.

When all the turf grass has been removed, the soil will need to be assessed and amended. If drainage is good and soil texture feels soft and crumbly, all that is needed is a bit of aged manure or compost to boost fertility. It is also a good idea to incorporate sharp builder's sand into soil whenever possible for its ability to create air spaces, bringing oxygen into the root zone. If the soil is heavy and dense, then the amendments should include the sand along with large amounts of whatever organic material is at hand. Leaves are by far the best choice, but grass clippings, peat moss and shredded black-and-white newspaper are also usable.

Starting the bed of your dreams

MAKING QUICK AND EASIER BEDS

Bed-making purists will have an argument with this method, but it avoids the agony of turf grass removal. When time and labor are unavailable to remove the grass, the bed can be built right over it, effectively smothering the turf.

First, mow the grass very short. Then cover the area of the new bed with eight to ten thicknesses of black-and-white newspaper (no color pages), trimming off parts that cross over the established new line. Onto the new bed, spread topsoil amended with aged manure, peat moss and builder's sand to an evenly distributed depth of 12 to 18 inches (30 to 45 cm). Sprinkle moderately with water to settle the surface of the new soil, then allow the new bed to sit for a few days before planting. The level will begin to sink, and over six weeks it will go down substantially.

The newspaper layers and weight of new soil will smother the grass and it will not reappear. Newsprint is a good source of organic material and it will compost under the bed, eventually to be consumed by worms. The new bed will be slightly elevated after it has finished sinking, but only enough to give good presentation to the plants in it. When the bed is planted and beginning to settle, use a blunt-nosed spade to cut a sharp edge all around it to separate it from the surrounding lawn.

SOLAR POWER

Areas of turf grass that are in bright sunlight can be made into a planting bed by solarization. This process uses the heat of sunlight to "cook" the grass and make it softer and more easily removed.

In late spring or early summer, mow the grass very short over the area to be treated and

Finding a way in

Maintaining a planted bed can be troublesome if there is no easy access to plants. Tiptoeing through the mass of growing things compacts the soil and often causes unavoidable damage to delicate buds and stems. If you place stepping stones strategically behind plants, you will find getting around and finding a perch much easier. Beds that run along a fence or property line should also have a narrow pathway between the bed and fence, allowing maintenance from behind the plants.

Utilitarian stepping stones can be developed into a design feature by setting them close enough to make a rambling pathway through the bed. A path is an invitation to take a walk through the plants, seeing them up close and from more interesting perspectives. Special rewards for those bothering to make the journey into the bed can be hidden from viewers on the outside. A collection of rockery plants set against the back of a boulder, or a small piece of statuary partially concealed in a clump of ferns, can be set along the path to be discovered by those who venture through.

cover it with a thick sheet or two of clear plastic, holding the edges firmly down with bricks or long boards. Keep the plastic in place for six weeks. The vegetation will first turn yellow, and then brown when the heat has killed the grass and weeds. The dead sod will be partially decomposed and quick to remove.

DON'T WASTE VALUABLE REAL ESTATE
Soil and turf grass that have been dug out during a garden renovation have great value, and every effort should be made to save them. What may seem like a mountain of soil is quickly diminished when you spread it 1 to 2 inches (2.5 to 5 cm) thick over your planting areas.

Turf grass is a valuable compost ingredient, containing all the essential elements for manufacturing premium compost. Nitrogen and moisture from the green blades, carbon from the crowns and roots, and micro-organisms in the adhering soil all work together to make their own lovely mix. Pile the sod green-side-down in an out of the way corner (where the pile can be quite high) or under the low branches of a large tree. Simply leave it there to decompose, and in a year there will be a pile of good-quality loamy soil with bits of grass growing on the sides. Remove the grass and use this premium soil where needed in the garden.

Planning the bed

Good garden design is a tricky business, and it is no easier when applied to a single border or bed. Experts can offer useful opinions to guide important choices, but if your bed is planted to please your own senses and perceptions, then that is good personal design and no one could have done it better. Some level of recognizable design can be accomplished by following trend-driven interests, like deep English perennial borders, or Southwestern grass landscapes. But the most genuinely successful garden design is the unique expression of one gardener.

The approval of others is welcome and appreciated, but it can never substitute for the confidence that comes from doing what you like in your own private space. It is difficult to move away from popular and admired images, but the best route to defining a personal style is to plant what gives pleasure. Good design rarely happens quickly; it evolves.

Narrow beds and borders might be short on space, but can hold a special plant treasure. The corner of this garage is anchored by an unusual Japanese maple, Acer japonicum *'Maiku Jaku' (zone 5), meaning 'dancing peacock'. The fanciful name reflects the several ornamental features – bold lacy foliage, white and maroon flowers, purple keys and flame-red autumn color. This is a handy place to make more of less with an impromptu wire trellis for morning glory vines and billowing clumps of yellow fumitory,* Corydalis lutea *(zone 5). The yellow corydalis blooms all summer, prefers light shade and seeds itself into nooks and crannies where nothing else will grow.*

From that perspective, the task is not so much making choices from a variety of recognized styles but understanding what basic forms, colors and fragrances you find personally pleasing. Our dislikes are quickly discovered; recognizing what our preferences are is slower. A useful exercise is to make a list of plants you pleasurably remember. Include childhood plants and flowers, glimpses of something notable frequently passed along a bus route, particularly enjoyable blossoms from a previous residence and anything coveted in a neighbor's garden. The point is not to acquire all these specimens but rather to look for the general qualities that made them memorable. This may reveal an appreciation of deep color, or an interest in flowering shrubs. These are the values inherent in good personal design, and they will be strong guidelines in your plant choices for new beds and borders.

Adapting your general interests to the specific light and moisture conditions of your garden will require some research with books, a willingness to compromise when necessary and a bit of experimentation. If you love cottage flowers like poppies, coneflowers and Michaelmas daisies but have a shady garden location, some effort is required to adjust these interests to the site. To get the color and natural forms you enjoy, try substituting leopard's bane (*Doronicum cordatum*, zone 4), goatsbeard (*Aruncus dioicus*, zone 3), turtlehead (*Chelone glabra*, zone 3), sweet rocket (*Hesperis matronalis*, zone 3), wild blue phlox (*Phlox divaricata*, zone 4), cardinal flower (*Lobelia cardinalis*, zone 2), obedient plant (*Physostegia virginiana*, zone 3) and feverfew (*Tanacetum parthenium* 'Aureum', zone 4). These shade-tolerant plants will satisfy a preference for bright colors, tall stems and varied petal forms.

A few practical concepts can be used to lay a groundwork. A planted bed will have a better winter appearance if it contains some low blossoming shrubs with woody stems set among the herbaceous plants that die to the ground with frost. The shrubs should be in scale with the bed dimensions. For smaller beds in city gardens, dwarf plants such as 'Little Princess' spirea (*Spiraea japonica* 'Little Princess', zone

Making old beds new again

Renovating an older bed is not much different from making a new one. First decide what plants are in good condition and worth keeping. Remove plants that have not grown well or are troubled by disease or insect problems. Healthy plants no longer of interest can be given to friends and neighbors who might enjoy them. The plants you keep may require dividing, and that will make more plants to be set into new locations or given away. Large shrubs in the bed can't be easily moved and will probably have to remain where they are, but perennials can be lifted and set in new locations that may better suit their light requirements. Dig out any weeds with a hand trowel, making sure to get their roots. Improve the soil with compost, manure and sand, then reshape the bed if you choose and give it a sharp edge all around. Finally, consider whether woody structural plants are needed at each end, or low flowering shrubs for the middle section. All that's left is the big question: what would you like to plant?

4), 'Nikko' deutzia (*Deutzia crenata* 'Nikko', zone 6) and dwarf flowering quince (*Chaenomeles* x *superba*, zone 4) are all suitable.

Ornamental beds need strong anchoring plants at each end to give balance and a sense of fixture in the landscape. Woody plants with vertical lines can be combined with plants with lower, spreading structures to create some weight at both ends of the bed. Permanent vertical features also give the bed dimension in more than one plane, relieving the flatness of the bed's appearance in winter. This is a good opportunity to introduce evergreen material that will have strong presence in all seasons. Conifers can be chosen for their

dwarf size and narrow pyramidal growth. For smaller beds, a cluster of three 'Green Mountain' boxwood (*Buxus microphylla* var. *koreana* 'Green Mountain', zone 5) is a good choice, with strong vertical lines that can easily be clipped into an informal cone shape between 24 and 36 inches (60 to 90 cm) in height. A larger bed could accommodate two dwarf Alberta spruce (*Picea glauca* var. *albertiana* 'Conica', zone 4) with their consistent cone shape and plush texture.

Small beds look best with just one tall anchoring plant set to one side rather than in the middle. Choices for a vertical feature include a small weeping tree such as 'Walker' cutleaf weeping caragana (*Caragana arborescens* 'Walker', zone 2), which has delicate ferny foliage and bright yellow flowers in spring. Low bun-shaped conifers like nest spruce (*Picea abies* 'Nidiformis', zone 3) and globe blue spruce (*Picea pungens* 'Glauca Globosa', zone 2) will spread to 5 feet (1.5 m) and so need a bit of room, but mini-spreaders like Little Gem spruce (*Picea abies* 'Little Gem', zone 3) and golden Japanese yew (*Taxus cuspidata* 'Aurescens', zone 4) will stay within a diameter of 24 to 36 inches (60 to 90 cm), and two or three can be grouped together.

Dividing monster hostas

Hostas that are left undisturbed for many years can become very large. They are exciting garden plants when left this way, but you can divide them into armies of smaller plants to make effective ground cover for large areas. This is best accomplished in autumn, or in spring when just the bud tips are showing. If the plant is divided when in full leaf, it will survive, but the foliage will be severely wilted and will not recover during the growing season.

Hostas tend to grow from a central crown outward in a big mass. Some smaller divisions may be easily dislodged from the sides, but often the central mass does not break apart easily. Less damage is done and more plants result from using a clean, sharp knife rather than a spade to divide the crown. If the plant is very large, a small flexible pruning saw will also do a neat and adequate job. Try to cut or saw through the crown so that several clusters of buds or foliage are contained within each piece. Dust the sections of cut crown that contain raw white tissue with powdered sulfur before replanting.

Using transplant solution

New plants going from a container into the ground and those divided from large perennial plants experience shock to the root system

80

Dividing perennials

Early autumn is an ideal time to divide perennials. Most perennial plants need to be divided every three to four years. Crowded clumps will have fewer blossoms and may be dead at the center of the clump.

- Plan to divide perennials on an overcast day to reduce stress from direct sunlight. Cut back the stems to 3 inches (7.5 cm) and use a small spade or garden fork to loosen the plant in the soil. Work at getting under the plant from four sides and lift the root ball upward and out of the soil.

- Plants like hosta and phlox form a thick central crown with small offshoots around the sides. The small outer plants can be gently separated by hand. The central crown can be cut into sections, each containing a cluster of crowns, using a long knife blade.

- Plants with fleshy roots like daylilies and peonies can be gently pulled or cut into sections, each with at least two eyes or buds. Iris rhizomes can also be cut into individual sections, each with a fan of leaves or growth point. Dahlias can be separated by cutting down through the stem to preserve an eye on each tuber.

- Old sections of roots and crowns from the middle of the clump should be discarded, even if they are still alive, and the younger, more vigorous sections from the exterior saved for replanting.

- Set the plant sections into holes at the same depth they were growing before division, and water them in with a fertilizer transplant solution or mix a generous handful of bone meal into the hole to encourage root growth.

- When the ground freezes, mulch the new divisions with 2 inches (5 cm) of leaf litter to prevent frost from heaving them out of the ground.

when they're replanted. Growth is suspended for one to three weeks while the newly divided root systems grow into the new hole and containerized plants adjust to the change in soil temperature. These processes can be sped along with transplant solution to water the plants into their new positions.

Garden centers sell two forms of transplant solution that are easily mixed in a watering can. One is a liquid concentrate with a nutrient formula of 5-15-5 and contains indolebutyric acid, a synthetic rooting hormone to encourage root growth. Another transplant fertilizer is sold as water-soluble crystals with a formula of 10-52-10 and contains a large amount of phosphorus that also promotes root growth. Organic bone meal, 0-11-0, is an organic source of phosphorus, and a generous handful can be mixed into each planting hole to stimulate rooting.

Evergreen plants for small beds

Adam's needle, *Yucca filamentosa*, zone 4, height 30 inches (75 cm), spread 24 inches (60 cm)

Bristlecone pine, *Pinus aristata*, zone 2, height 8 feet (2.4 m), spread 48 inches (120 cm)

Degroot's Spire cedar, *Thuja occidentalis* 'Degroot's Spire', zone 3, height 8 feet (2.4 m), spread 24 inches (60 cm)

Dwarf balsam fir, *Abies balsamea* 'Nana', zone 5, height 24 inches (60 cm), spread 36 inches (90 cm)

Dwarf hinoki false cypress, *Chamaecyparis obtusa* 'Nana Gracilis', zone 5, height 36 inches (90 cm), spread 36 inches (90 cm)

Dwarf Japanese yew, *Taxus cuspidata* 'Nana', zone 4, height 36 inches (90 cm), spread 36 inches (90 cm)

Emerald cedar, *Thuja occidentalis* 'Emerald', zone 4, height 10 feet (3 m), spread 36 inches (90 cm)

Emerald Gaiety euonymus, *Euonymus fortunei* 'Emerald Gaiety', zone 5, height 36 inches (90 cm), spread 36 inches (90 cm)

Gold Tip euonymus, *Euonymus fortunei* 'Gold Tip', zone 5, height 36 inches (90 cm), spread 36 inches (90 cm)

Golden Globe cedar, *Thuja occidentalis* 'Golden Globe', zone 3, height 36 inches (90 cm), spread 36 inches (90 cm)

Golden Japanese yew, *Taxus cuspidata* 'Aurescens', zone 4, height 12 inches (30 cm), spread 36 inches (90 cm)

Green Mountain boxwood, *Buxus microphylla* var. *koreana* 'Green Mountain', zone 5, height 48 inches (120 cm), spread 36 inches (90 cm)

Holmstrup cedar, *Thuja occidentalis* 'Holmstrup', zone 3, height 7 feet (2 m), spread 36 inches (90 cm)

Jervis dwarf hemlock, *Tsuga canadensis* 'Jervis', zone 4, height 36 inches (90 cm), spread 36 inches (90 cm)

Koster's false cypress, *Chamaecyparis obtusa* 'Kosteri', zone 4, height 48 inches (120 cm), spread 36 inches (90 cm)

Little Gem spruce, *Picea abies* 'Little Gem', zone 3, height 18 inches (45 cm), spread 24 inches (60 cm)

Little Giant globe cedar, *Thuja occidentalis* 'Little Giant', zone 3, height 36 inches (90 cm), spread 36 inches (90 cm)

Miniature black spruce, *Picea mariana* 'Ericoides', zone 2, height 24 inches (60 cm), spread 36 inches (90 cm)

Mountain Fire pieris, *Pieris japonica* 'Mountain Fire', zone 6, height 36 inches (90 cm), spread 36 inches (90 cm)

Rheingold cedar, *Thuja occidentalis* 'Rheingold', zone 3, height 48 inches (120 cm), spread 36 inches (90 cm)

Sunkist cedar, *Thuja occidentalis* 'Sunkist', zone 2, height 6 feet (1.8 m), spread 36 inches (90 cm)

Sunproof gold thread cypress, *Chamaecyparis pisifera* 'Filifera Aurea Nana', zone 5, height 36 inches (90 cm), spread 36 inches (90 cm)

Sunspot euonymus, *Euonymus fortunei* 'Sunspot', zone 5, height 36 inches (90 cm), spread 36 inches (90 cm)

Weeping trees for small beds

Sargents weeping hemlock, *Tsuga canadensis* 'Pendula', zone 4, height 5 feet (1.5 m), spread 7 feet (2 m)

Walker cutleaf weeping caragana, *Caragana arborescens* 'Walker', zone 2, height 5 feet (1.5 m), spread 5 feet (1.5 m)

Weeping European larch, *Larix decidua* 'Pendula', zone 4, height 5 feet (1.5 m), spread 5 feet (1.5 m)

Weeping goat willow, *Salix caprea* 'Pendula', zone 4, height 5 feet (1.5 m), spread 5 feet (1.5 m)

Weeping Japanese ch1erry, *Prunus serrulata* 'Kiku-shidare-zakura', zone 6, height 8 feet (2.4 m), spread 6 feet (1.8 m)

Weeping white pine, *Pinus strobus* 'Pendula', zone 4, height 8 feet (2.4 m), spread 6 feet (1.8 m)

Placement hierarchy

The standard rule of "tall forms toward the back and short forms to the front" is a fundamental method of plant placement. Lining plants up in this way gives a rigid order to the landscape and a full-view, one-dimensional picture. The effect is very much like a picture postcard, with everything neatly in place. Such a low-risk arrangement holds no surprises and is always predictable. And what's wrong with that? Sometimes it's reassuring to know what the view is before the eye falls on it.

But other gardeners like the view to be a bit more unpredictable and dangerous. Perhaps the plants could be slightly out of linear order, or something tall and fabulous may have found its way to the front of the bed. This is a bit of an outlaw approach, but some rules just beg to be broken. Transgressing lines of height can be a dynamic tool if the right plants get into the right places.

The commonsense approach is to bring forward anything tall and slender enough to be a "see-through" plant. Qualifications for this special treatment are plants with aesthetic value for the entire season, such as tall columbines (*Aquilegia* spp., zone 4), meadow rues (*Thalictrum* spp., zone 5), the various bugbanes (*Cimicifuga* spp., zone 4) and penstemons (zone 5), all plants that have wonderful flowers but also attractive foliage from spring to autumn. See-through candidates are tall but not dense and won't block the view of plants behind. Tall bulbous lilies are also good for placement near the front, as are Japanese anemones (*Anemone* x *hybrida*, zone 5) and cardinal flowers (*Lobelia cardinalis*, zone 3). Oriental poppies wouldn't work right at the front: although their flowers are tall and stunningly beautiful, their foliage is a ratty mess. They need something in front of them to hide their miserable leaves after blooming.

Planting geometry

The sight of plants in rigidly straight rows is reminiscent of Victorian precision planting. While demonstrating great skill on the part of the gardener, straight lines do little to emphasize the naturalism of a planting. Unless the intention is to line a walkway or make a long edging with one variety of plant, the straight-line formations are best saved for French parterre and vegetable gardening.

Perennial plants enjoy company in a congenial and relaxed grouping based on triangle formations. Setting plants of the same kind in a three-point formation with space to grow between them allows plants to fill in and mass together, making a pleasantly generous clump of foliage and flowers within an informal and relaxed setting. When planning for a space where more than one plant can be accommodated, try to acquire plants in odd-numbered groups — three, five, seven and so on — and set them in triangular arrangements with shared sides. Plants like foxglove, astilbe and coral bells will look best in odd-numbered arrangements.

How deep?

The look of fullness in a perennial border is created by layering lines, or laneways, of plants one beside another. Think of the border as three highway lanes, allowing for tall, medium and low plants. Each lane of planting needs to be 24 inches (60 cm) wide to allow for the development of plant clumps; the lane for tall plants might need to be expanded to 36 inches

Plants with attitude and altitude

Some perennials are big and interesting enough that one specimen plant can stand on its own in a border. Plants with this much attitude and 5 feet (150 cm) in height include the great airy burst of sea kale (*Crambe cordifolia*, zone 6, sun), notoriously spreading plume poppy (*Macleaya cordata*, zone 4, sun to part shade), the juvenile red foliage of ornamental rhubarb (*Rheum palmatum* 'Atrosanguineum', zone 5, sun to part shade) and the deep purple umbels of biennial purple angelica (*Angelica archangelica* 'Gigas', zone 4, sun to part shade).

The towering white spires of culver's root (*Veronicastrum virginicum*, zone 3, sun to part shade) and the trembling fragility of meadow rue (*Thalictrum rochebrunianum*, zone 5, sun to part shade) are more slender forms, and two or three plants could be grouped to make a dense mass. Meadow rues are challenging to grow in warm regions, and only the cultivar 'Hewitt's Double' (*Thalictrum delavayi*, zone 4) is reliable in southern gardens, where it will need some shade and a thick mulch over its roots.

(90 cm) if particularly bushy plants are chosen. Three laneways, or a total width of 6 to 7 feet (1.8 to 2 m), is the minimum needed for a border with some appearance of depth and fullness. More and wider laneways increase the impression of fullness. Using tall see-through plants near the front of the border helps to create an illusion of greater depth, as does a curved line to the edge that can swing out deeply where possible and move in when space is narrow. If the width of the garden is less than 25 feet (7.5 m), it's possible to make one generous border, 6 to 8 feet (1.8 to 2.4 m) deep, down the sunniest side that allows for a deep planting of perennials, and to grow flowering vines on the opposite side.

When a bed is less than 5 feet wide (1.5 m), it is better to make a planting of something with season-long interest, with a small edging plant in front. This could be a traditional peony border with an edging of annual sweet alyssum, or tuberous begonias with a perennial border of 'White Nancy' spotted dead nettle (*Lamium maculatum* 'White Nancy', zone 5).

Banking on it

To make a narrow border appear wider, bank the soil so that it rises 6 to 8 inches (15 to 20 cm) from the center of the bed to the back. This will give the impression of greater density and stronger presentation to the plants elevated at the rear, although the change in level should not be immediately noticeable.

A gardener with building skills constructed this generous gazebo with room for sofas and chairs. The planting bed of mixed annuals and perennials bordering the informal path helps to balance the large scale of the structure and gracefully integrate the summerhouse into the landscape. Tall plants like pink cleome, orange tithonia and the creamy heads of hydrangea add height and mass to the bed. The green lace-leaf Japanese maple, evergreen spruce and young anjelica tree (Aralia elata, zone 5) are prominent anchoring features in four seasons.

Planting

Plants are bought in all kinds of conditions. Plants in containers are the most adaptable, having the advantage of fully developed root systems and conscientious care in a nursery setting. They are available throughout the growing season and can go into the ground immediately or be held for a while until the bed is ready.

Pest watch

When getting ready to plant new perennials from a nursery, have a look to be sure the plants are not accompanied by whiteflies or aphids. If you see some, let the nursery know, and spray them thoroughly with insecticidal soap and rubbing alcohol (one tablespoon (50mL) of rubbing alcohol mixed into every one cup (250mL) of insecticidal soap)

Feed them

It takes a lot of carbohydrate energy to manufacture flowers, and feeding newly installed perennials considerably enhances their ability to perform quickly. Be sure to amend their soil with compost or aged manure when preparing the planting hole, and use a liquid transplant solution to water them immediately after planting.

If the plants are waiting for the site to be prepared, keep them in shade. The plastic or fiber containers they live in can collect heat and cook the roots. Providing moisture is also essential, but hold off on any fertilizers while they are in their pots. If you look after them well, they will make the transition into permanent locations in the ground without any interruption to their growth.

Balled and burlapped plants are dug from growing fields in the spring and autumn, but not during the main summer growing months. Their root systems are tightly wrapped in burlap and tied; if the plant is very large, a wire basket may hold the burlapped root ball.

Perennial plants delivered by mail may arrive in pots with green stems and foliage. Other mail-order plants, especially large woody ones, which most often arrive with bare roots and in a dormant condition, have been kept in cold storage to prevent them from growing. They will have the unhopeful appearance of brown roots and little, if any, green foliage. Their discouraging demeanor may lead you to think they can be roughly handled, but this is a mistake. Dormant plants possess all that is needed to grow to their potential and should be treated carefully.

Plants are shipped in this condition most often in spring, and may arrive slightly ahead of the season. If it is only a matter of two or three days' wait before they can go into the ground, check inside the package to be sure there is no obvious sign of mold on the roots, then rewrap them and keep them in an

Renovating an old garden bed

Small garden beds can be renovated all at one time. Larger beds can be divided into sections and the renovation accomplished in stages over a longer time.

- Determine what plants are to be eliminated from the bed. Remove plants that do not grow well in the available light and moisture conditions, as well as any plants subject to insect and disease problems.

- Plants that are to be retained should be carefully lifted using asmall spade or garden fork and set into a container or plastic bag. A kiddy pool or baby bath will hold many plants in a healthy state for a short time. Divide any plants with old or crowded crowns. Cover plant roots to prevent drying out.

- Edge the bed and renew its shape, making changes to enlarge or modify the area.

- Remove all weeds, dead roots, sticks and debris.

- Improve the soil with organic amendments such as compost, aged manure, shredded leaves, peat moss and sand.

- Reset the plants into the renovated bed, working from the back toward the front, or if the bed is an island, from the middle out to the edges. Water each plant into its new position. Use transplant fertilizer solution or bone meal in the holes of plants that have been divided.

- Mulch the bed with 2 inches (5 cm) of shredded leaves or bark.

unheated garage or shed. If planting is delayed any longer, plant them in containers with soil, give them regular water and keep them in a shady spot.

A movable nursery

When you must keep mail-order plants for a week or more before they can go into the ground, pot them into a container with soil, water them and place them in a shady location.

When many small perennial plants have arrived, an alternative method is to prepare a "gro-bag" for them. Purchase a large bag of soilless mix (peat moss, vermiculite and perlite), poke several drainage holes in one flat side and lay the bag, hole-side-down, on a boot mat or large plastic tray. In the top cut an X for each plant. Insert the plants into these holes, carefully burying the root systems into the soilless mix. Water each plant with warm water and set the temporary nursery in a bright place, but out of direct sunlight that could heat up the bag. Plants can be kept this way, indoors or out, for several weeks.

Planting new perennials

- Be sure the location provides adequate light and moisture for the new plant.

- Groom the plant carefully, removing old stem stubs, dead leaves around the base and any spent blossoms or seed heads.

- Prepare a hole for the plant, amending the soil with compost or aged manure. Dig the hole twice as wide as the plant's root ball and loosen the soil in the bottom. Organic fertilizers such as blood, bone and kelp meal can be mixed into the hole.

- Most perennial plants arrive in plastic containers, but some are grown in fiberboard pots. Despite their organic material, fiber pots will not decompose underground and must be removed.

- Spread your fingers across the top of the pot and turn the plant upside-down, supporting it with your hand. Gently tap the bottom of the pot to loosen the plant. If the plant will not slide out, lay the container on its side and gently press on the sides, then try again to remove the plant. Do not pull on the stem or foliage.

- New perennial plants may have been in their pots for a long time. Examine the sides of the root ball for circling or congested roots. Gently tease these roots out, loosening the root ball. If roots are greatly congested it may be necessary to cut them along the sides of the root ball to encourage new root growth into the soil.

- Set the plant into its hole and water it in with a transplant fertilizer solution.

Bigger is quicker

When buying perennial plants, the general rule is the larger the pot, the bigger the price, and the quicker the plant will become established and flower.

Perennial plants in 4-inch (100-mm) pots may send up only a solitary sample of their flowering ability in the first season. But during that time they will be busy making new roots and enlarging the plant's crown so that the following year the display will be much larger.

Buying larger divisions in gallon containers is a way of getting a fuller floral display in the first season. The larger containers accommodate a more developed root system and a more mature crown with greater energy potential.

Planting in frost-free regions

Planting perennials in warm regions requires slightly different timing. Autumn is the best season for dividing plants or planting new ones because of the potential for an extended winter period of cool temperatures for new root growth. Planting in spring is possible, but with the imminent big heat soon to come, you will have to water perennials constantly from late spring through summer. Plants installed in spring absolutely must be mulched with an organic material to help conserve moisture and lower soil temperature in the root zone.

Short memories

Despite the excitement of acquiring each new plant, gardeners sometimes have short memories. Plant labels can help you remember what is where, but they are not without difficulties. Plastic stick labels are the most affordable in large quantities, but become brittle if exposed to the elements for very long. The information they carry is also likely to fade. And despite the necessary service they provide, it's hard to justify their presence in the aesthetic picture.

To avoid later frustration, write the plants' names on the sticks with a felt-tipped indelible marker. Bury the sticks at the base of each plant to protect them from the sun and increase their longevity. (Burying them on the shaded north side of every plant to avoid direct sun will also help them last longer.) Leave the tips aboveground so they can be seen in spring before the plants are up.

*Sunflowers sown by an industrious squirrel demonstrate the ability of plants to push through every crack and crevice. Seeds of perennial oregano and annual sweet alyssum have also taken hold and flourish in the concrete. This resourceful gardener makes use of every growing space on a busy city corner, combining tomatoes with self-sown plants and pots of annual coleus and variegated flowering maple (*Abutilon hybridium spp.*).*

Annuals and perennials

In northern climates, many plants are grown as annuals with a life expectancy of less than 12 months, but the same plant in a southern frost-free region could be perennial, living for several years. The ability of plants to tolerate frost in cold regions is the key to long life in the garden.

Category descriptions in plant catalogues indicate plant life cycles in each region. Annual plants live 12 months or less, completing their life cycle within one growing season. Biennial plants live 18 to 24 months, growing their root system and a rosette of foliage in the first summer, becoming dormant over the winter and coming into bloom during the second summer. Perennial plants will live indefinitely and have the ability to withstand varying degrees of frost.

Plant descriptions are often categorized in more complex ways, particularly in seed catalogues. Hardy annuals will tolerate light frost in spring and autumn, and will often self-seed in the garden. The seeds remain on the ground through the winter, until the fluctuating temperatures of warm days and cold nights in the early spring prompt germination. Larkspur, poppies, sweet alyssum, portulaca, calendula, love-in-a-mist, cosmos, nicotiana, cleome and pansies are some of the flowers that often return to the garden for many seasons, seeding themselves each year.

Half-hardy annuals have no frost tolerance but will withstand cool weather above the freezing point. Petunias, marigolds, geraniums and impatiens are in this category and must be started indoors each year or purchased as bedding plants.

Tender annuals are plants from tropical regions with no frost or cold tolerance. They will sulk if set outside too early, and don't grow well until night temperatures are above 50°F (10°C). Sunflowers, morning glories, zinnias, moonflower, coleus and caladium, and such vegetables as eggplant, peppers, squash and corn, all require warm soil and air temperatures.

Many perennials can tolerate deep frost, among them hostas, phlox and cranesbill geraniums. But others, like heliotrope and fuchsia, are classified as half-hardy or tender perennials and in colder zones are grown as annuals. Grown as perennials, they may require some protection from winter wind or a thick mulch covering when planted in regions at the edge of their hardiness zone. Their root systems are somewhat sensitive to deep frost, so they may need to be placed in a bed near a heated house wall to raise the winter soil temperature just enough to keep them from dying.

Short-lived perennials are plants with a predisposition to some form of environmental damage, often associated with moisture conditions, and they may live in the garden for two or three years before they disappear. Delphiniums can be short-lived and suffer from crown rot caused by winter wetness. Columbines may not stay long either, and are vulnerable to the energy-depleting columbine leaf miner.

Big cities, hot beds

Every gardener wants to grow plants that are comfortably within their hardiness zone. But it is also worthwhile to experiment with a few plants that are just slightly beyond their cold-hardiness region. Some may have ancestral genes that will help them adapt and flourish despite the low temperatures.

Temperature is the greatest environmental influence on the growth and development of plants. Cities tend to be several degrees warmer in winter than their surrounding regions, because of the heat accumulated from the burning of so much fuel in a concentrated area. This accumulation of heat creates a slight hot house effect, making it possible to grow plants at the extreme edge of their hardiness zone. The same plants would be more vulnerable to winter cold in the suburbs just beyond the city.

Annual plants: endless summer

All any gardener wants is masses of flowers beginning in the first warm days of spring and lasting until the snow flies. And with annual plants, this is not so difficult to achieve.

Cold-hardy perennial plants live indefinitely in the garden but bloom for only a few weeks each season. They return dependably every year, and the price of their permanent status is a short period of blossom. Annual plants are in place for a much shorter time, just the span of one season, before they are killed by frost. Yet they will bloom almost from their arrival in spring or early summer until hard frost cuts them down in late autumn.

Annual plants allow you to change color

Annual plants for light shade

Baby blue eyes, *Nemophilia* spp.
Begonia spp.
Browallia, *Browallia speciosa*
Coleus spp.
Impatiens spp.
Lobelia, *Lobelia erinus*
Monkey flower, *Mimulus* spp.
Nicotiana, *Nicotiana* spp.
Painted tongue, *Salpiglossis sinuata*
Pansies, *Viola* spp.
Wishbone flower, *Torenia fournieri*

schemes quickly and supply a constant show of flowers to bridge the gaps between fading perennials in beds and borders. In containers, annuals can soften patios, decks and doorsteps and are the mainstays for plantings in window boxes and hanging baskets. Tall plants like cleome, spreading petunias and draping diascia and lobelia adapt to many design uses in arrangements to last the whole season.

Some plants are true annuals, growing from seeds sown in late winter, producing foliage and flowers, manufacturing a crop of seeds and dying within a twelve-month period. But many frost-tender perennial plants, such as gazania and fuchsia, are grown and used as annuals in northern regions. These tender perennials have the capability to live much longer in southern regions, but their susceptibility to frost is the limiting factor in the north.

ANNUAL TIPS

Annual plants are grown for one season. Plant them in spring and remove them in autumn. They can be planted in containers and window boxes, and also directly in garden beds. When planted in the ground, the additional space for root growth allows the plants to become taller and fuller than identical plants grown in root-confining containers.

Annuals you purchase in spring may have arrived directly from a warm greenhouse. It will be necessary to harden them off and gradually introduce them to outdoor temperatures and sunlight. Put them outdoors in shade just for an hour the first day, and increase the time outside on the following days. At night they can go into a garage or be covered with several sheets of newspaper. Give them just a short period of direct sunlight at first, and increase the exposure each day. The plants should be well acclimatized in seven to ten days.

You can plant annuals outside when the night temperatures are above 50°F (10°C). Remove the plants from their plastic cell packs by gently pressing on the bottom of each cell and pushing the plant up. Never pull the plant by the stem. If the plants can't be pushed out, tear the side of the plastic cell. Plants that have been in their cell packs for too long will have a thick accumulation of fibrous roots on the outside of the root ball. Gently

Self-seeding annuals

Some annual plants produce seed with enough cold-hardiness to remain viable in the soil over winter. The seeds respond to the oscillating temperatures of warm days and frosty nights in earliest spring and spontaneously germinate. These self-sown plants will be sturdy and large, with many flowers produced through the growing season. If there is a self-seeding annual you always want to have in the garden, let it go to seed and propagate itself. Amongst the plants that will seed themselves are:

California poppy, *Eschscholzia*
Morning glory, *Ipomoea* spp.
Nicotiana, *Nicotiana* spp.
Pot marigold, *Calendula officinalis*
Spider flower, *Cleome* spp.
Sweet alyssum, *Alyssum maritimum*

tear these roots to open up the root ball and allow new roots to grow into the soil. A large root system is the most important factor in successful blossom production.

Plants can be spaced very closely in containers, 4 or 5 inches (10 or 12.5 cm) apart, or more widely in the ground. The distance between plants will depend on their eventual size. Spreading plants like sweet alyssum and calendula should be planted 8 to 10 inches (20 to 23 cm) apart in the ground. But big plants like cosmos will need room to grow and should be spaced 14 to 18 inches (35 to 45 cm) apart.

Use a transplant fertilizer when setting plants out to get them off to a strong start. Annual plants want to produce their flowers quickly and can make a good show on their own, though you may want to feed them something extra for a big splash of blossoms. Use a fertilizer every three weeks with a higher middle number, say 5-10-5 or 15-30-15, to encourage root growth and bud set. All plants love fish emulsion fertilizers, but manufactured fertilizers are also effective.

Deadheading is very important if you want plants to keep pumping out flowers until hard frost. When blossoms die, plants begin to make seed heads that signal the end of flower production. To prevent this process, cut off blossoms just as they begin going brown. Monitor plants weekly and remove any browning leaves and dead or decaying tissue to prevent fungus infections.

If plants get too tall and lanky mid-season or seem exhausted, shear off one-third of their top growth and fertilize. They will put on new side growth, become bushier and produce more flower buds in two to three weeks.

Spring bulbs: getting up early

Spring bulbs lengthen the growing season and make good companion plants for early-blossoming shrubs. The earliest bulbs (*Eranthis, Iris reticulata* and *I. danfordiae*) are up and flowering in the snow long before perennial plants are in bud, and their form and substance are unlike any other in the garden. Making bulbs successful in your garden requires understanding what they need and developing a growing strategy.

Spring bulbs are purchased in early autumn and planted before hard frost. The small, or minor, bulbs such as crocus and scilla must be planted as soon as possible to prevent drying out, but large bulbs such as narcissus and tulips can be planted into November in the north. The bulbs you purchase in autumn contain the flower embryo for next spring, and require only a moist soil to form roots in and at least sixteen weeks of underground chilling.

The rule of green thumb is to plant bulbs three times their depth in the soil. Bulbs like a sandy soil with good drainage and are vulnerable to rot in heavy clay. If your soil is heavy, dig generous amounts of sharp sand into specific areas and cluster bulbs there. They look best when crowded together in a group, and

this will allow you to keep the digging to a minimum. Newly purchased bulbs have been heavily fertilized during their production and don't require any more feeding at planting time. Once in the moist soil they spontaneously grow roots and await their period of chilling.

The time to apply fertilizer is in spring when the foliage is about halfway up and before flower buds are showing. A basic granular fertilizer with low numbers, like 5-3-8 or 6-9-5, can be scratched into the soil around the bulbs and will help to insure that they return to blossom again next year. As soon as the flowers are finished and falling, cut off the heads to prevent seed formation and allow the

*Deep in an urban ravine spring bulbs and perennials bloom in early light. The first of the rhododendrons and azaleas are beginning to open, surrounded by emerging jack-in-the-pulpit (*Arisaema spp., *zone 4) and snowdrop anemones (*Anemone sylvestris, *zone 2). The lobed leaves of bloodroot (*Sanguinaria canadensis, *zone 3) are already well extended amidst white trilliums, hanging bells of guinea-hen flowers (*Fritillaria meleagris, *zone 3, hardy bulb) and yellow trout lilies (*Erythronium grandiflorum, *zone 5, hardy bulb). Farther up the steep path, clumps of yellow-flowered barrenwort (*Epimedium x versicolor *'Sulphureum', zone 4) are beginning to bloom and will make an effective ground cover when the dry slope is shaded by trees in summer.*

foliage to naturally ripen. The leaves will continue to live for another four to six weeks while making energy for next year's flower. Continue to water the bulbs while the foliage is still green. The large leaves of tulips and narcissus are a bit unsightly, but resist the temptation to tie them together in a neat knot – this will interfere with manufacturing energy. Planting bulbs behind daylilies usually works to hide the ripening foliage. The leaves can be removed when they are half brown. Be sure to cut the stems, not pull them, or the bulb might come out of the ground.

Bulb strategies

Spring sunlight warms the soil and signals bulbs to start growing, but the shade from large deciduous trees tends to keep the soil cold and the bulbs will be slow to start. Plant only the earliest bulbs, such as crocus and specie tulips, that can respond to warming sunlight before the tree leaves come out. Then plant woodland plants such as violets, hepatica, bloodroot and bleeding heart to complete the spring garden.

Bulbs planted in heavy garden soil often don't return well in subsequent years. Of the many categories of tulips available, the most reliably perennial is May-blooming Darwin tulips. It's a big category with lots of color selection, and it's possible to make a very nice spring garden with several kinds of Darwins in combination with perennial plants.

Hard stuff

Architectural elements can have a place in beds and borders. Bird baths, obelisks and ornamental trellis screens add depth and dimension to a garden bed and give the garden winter presence. A trellised arbor placed in the border is a strong vertical element and also provides an opportunity to embellish the structure with several ornamental flowering vines that bloom from spring to late autumn.

To stabilize an arbor standing in a bed, pound a 5-foot steel T-bar into the earth on each side at the back of the arbor. Use heavy wire to hold the arbor tightly to the bars.

Seeing colors

The tyranny of pink

You may have noticed the vise-like grip of pink on the gardening consciousness in the past two decades. The pinkness of so many petals has quite overwhelmed the strident tones of traditional flowers like red zinnias and orange tiger lilies and influenced plant hybridizers to breed pink selections of these heritage dazzlers. Where has all this pinkness come from? The late British author Thalassa Cruso often referred to "Garden of Eden Pink," the original color at the genetic base of so many hybridized flowering plants. It seems that in the natural landscapes of rain forests, prairies and mountain slopes, much that blooms is pink.

Pink has adapted well to contemporary gardens and flooded the plant market with rapturous shades from the palest shell pink of the 'New Dawn' climbing rose, to the Day-Glo saturation of magenta-pink rose campion (*Lychnis coronaria*, zone 5). The diversity of pink hues is so voluminous that it is possible to make an entire garden in pink without realizing the palette is confined to one color family.

But what does pinkness do for a small city garden, except make it predictable? The limitation of planting space in a city garden invites a statement of more dramatic tone. A small garden is an opportunity to do something out of character with the neighborhood but in keeping with the gardener's true colors in a dynamic, possibly changing and sometimes humorous way. Color is foremost an expression of temperament, and a very handy medium for expressing one's current frame of mind.

Traditional guidelines for use of color focus on using hot colors sparingly and whitewashing them with pastels. However, much can be said about choosing "complementary" colors like purple and yellow and about avoiding "clashing" colors like red and orange, but if the garden is to have any relevance to you, its maker, it must reflect the hues of your character and temperament.

The rehabilitation of orange

Long the preferable color in citrus fruit but otherwise banned from polite society since the late 1970s, orange is making a vibrant reappearance in ornamental flowering plants. New canna lilies, tulips, pansies, impatiens and begonias are once again flaunting this deepest of sun shades. Christened with a new name to dispel lingering aspersions, orange is

Pink and proud of it! There's no arguing with success when a predominantly pink bed is artfully displayed in a summer landscape. This old-fashioned border of perennial phlox and lilies is banded with a ribbon of annual impatiens under a canopy of mature trees. Phlox is available in a broader color range than any other perennial plant, but almost everyone shares the enthusiasm for masses of it in pink. A long border like this is always a happy event when plants are groomed, the edge is sharply cut and a generous curving line runs the length of the garden. This resourceful gardener has stashed a supply of peat moss along the stepping-stone service path behind the border to keep all that pink glowing through heat and drought.

now "apricot," and it is much in demand for pairing up with strong blues and purples. This long-awaited epiphany in the public color consciousness brings the good news that strong colors are back and available in many plant forms.

Other vibrant colors, such as jewel tones of scarlet cardinal flower and deep blue gentians, were until recently thought of as brash. These deep and resonant tones are now welcome luxuries to city gardeners overdosed with decades of pale blossoms.

Some gardeners with wayward intentions lean toward the hottest combinations of intensely saturated red pigments paired with electric violets, or the flashy partnership of deep and dusky purples with many of the lime-green and chartreuse flowers now available. Still unimaginable in some communities, black is a color now reproduced in accessible plants like pansies, poppies, carnations, hollyhocks and columbines. Plants with gray foliage or palest yellow flowers are often the soothing counterpoints in these intense relationships, along with a scattering of variegated cream-and-green leaves.

Woody shrubs with cream to white flowers

White forsythia, *Abeliophyllum distichum,* zone 5, sun
Common pearlbush, *Exochorda racemosa,* zone 4, sun
Star magnolia, *Magnolia stellata,* zone 5, sun to part shade
Common white lilac, *Syringa vulgaris alba* and hybrids, zone 3, sun
Serviceberry, *Amelanchier canadensis,* zone 4, sun to part shade
Winter honeysuckle, *Lonicera fragrantissima,* zone 5, sun
Lily-of-the-valley bush, *Pieris japonica,* zone 6, part to full shade
White rhododendron, *Rhododendron* species and hybrids, zone 4, part shade
Black jetbead, *Rhodotypos scandens,* zone 4, sun to shade
Slender deutzia, *Deutzia gracilis,* zone 5, sun to part shade
Chinese loropetalum *Loropetalum chinense,* zone 9, sun to part shade
Viburnum species and hybrids, zone 5, sun to part shade

Cape jasmine, *Gardenia jasminoides,* zone 9, sun to part shade
Virginia sweetspire, *Itea virginica,* zone 5, sun to shade
Snowmound spirea, *Spiraea nipponica,* 'Snowmound' zone 4, sun to part shade
Mock orange hybrids, *Philadelphus,* zone 4, sun to part shade
Annabelle hydrangea, *Hydrangea arborescens* 'Annabelle', and Peegee hydrangea, *H. paniculata* 'Grandiflora', zone 4, sun to part shade
Oak-leaf hydrangea, *Hydrangea quercifolia,* zone 6, sun to part shade
White butterfly bush, *Buddleia davidii* 'White Profusion', zone 5, sun
White crape myrtle, *Lagerstroemia indica,* zone 7, sun
White rose of Sharon, *Hibiscus syriacus,* zone 6, sun to part shade
False spirea, *Sorbaria sorbifolia,* zone 4, sun to shade
White summersweet, *Clethra alnifolia* 'Paniculata', zone 4, sun to part shade
Japanese camellia, *Camellia japonica,* zone 7, part shade

Perennial plants with shades of blue flowers

Violets, *Viola* spp., zone 4, sun to shade

Blue moss phlox, *Phlox subulata* hybrids, zone 4, sun

Woodland phlox, *Phlox divaricata*, zone 4, part to full shade

Blue summer phlox, *Phlox paniculata* hybrids, zone 5, sun to part shade

Jacob's ladder, *Polemonium caeruleum*, zone 4, sun to part shade

Creeping Jacob's ladder, *Polemonium reptans*, zone 4, part shade

Virginia bluebells, *Mertensia virginica*, zone 4, part to full shade

Siberian bugloss, *Brunnera macrophylla*, zone 4, part to full shade

Garden forget-me-not, *Myosotis sylvatica*, zone 5, sun to part shade

Blue lungwort, *Pulmonaria angustifolia*, zone 4, part to full shade

Blue Carpathian bellflower, *Campanula carpatica*, zone 4, sun to part shade

Clustered bellflower, *Campanula glomerata*, zone 3, sun to part shade

Peach-leaved bellflower, *Campanula persicifolia*, zone 4, sun to part shade

Rocky Mountain columbine, *Aquilegia caerulea*, zone 3, sun to part shade

Fan columbine, *Aquilegia flabellata*, zone 3, sun to part shade

Mountain bluet, *Centaurea montana*, zone 3, sun to part shade

Balloon flower, *Platycodon grandiflorus*, zone 3, sun to part shade

Lilac cranesbill, *Geranium himalayense*, zone 4, sun to part shade

Cranesbill, *Geranium pratense* 'Plenum Caeruleum', zone 4, sun to part shade

Blue Stoke's aster, *Stokesia laevis*, zone 5, sun

Great blue lobelia, *Lobelia siphilitica*, zone 4, sun to part shad

Pincushion flower, *Scabiosa caucasica* 'Fama', zone 3, sun to part shade

Big betony, *Stachys macrantha*, zone 4, sun to part shade

Perennial salvia, *Salvia superba*, zone 5, sun

Spike speedwell, *Veronica spicata* hybrids, zone 5, sun

False indigo, *Baptisia australis*, zone 4, sun to part shade

Willow gentian, *Gentiana asclepiadea*, zone 5, part shade

Crested gentian, *Gentiana septemfida*, zone 5, sun to part shade

Perennial flax, *Linum perenne*, zone 5, sun to part shade

Small globe thistle, *Echinops ritro*, zone 4, sun

Bluetop sea holly, *Eryngium alpinum*, zone 3, sun to part shade

Cupid's dart, *Catananche caerulea*, zone 6, sun

Virginia spiderwort, *Tradescantia* x *andersoniana*, zone 5, part shade

Blue leadwort, *Ceratostigma plumbaginoides*, zone 5, sun to part shade

Showing true colors

Choice brings its own dilemma and crisis of introspection. And your decisions might well be guided by what colors give satisfaction in the immediate season. One strategy is to use a permanent selection of flowering shrubs all chosen within the spectrum of white to cream blossoms as a background accompaniment to stronger seasonal plants that can be changed occasionally. Or a collection of blue-flowering perennials could be installed as the permanent collection with changing selections of annual plants each season.

Obsessive interest in a color can result in a monochromatic scheme of all-cool or all-hot tones in one planting area, such as the red border made by British gardener and author Christopher Lloyd at Great Dixter, or the famous white garden made in the early part of the twentieth century by Vita Sackville-West at Sissinghurst Castle, and these single-color gardens continue to be replicated. But it is not necessary for you to organize colors in such rigid ways, and each season's choices can be a radical departure from previous colors. The easy strategy is to choose colors that have immediate appeal, enjoy them until interest shifts, then make a change. Just as temperament changes with age and experience, so will color choices. There is a time for absolute pinkness, and then the gardener gratefully moves on.

Putting it all together

Making plant associations

A favorite game in horticultural circles is to place plants in creative and complementary groupings, often referred to as marriages. It is a challenging pursuit, requiring not a little skill to recognize the effective features of plants and find complementary partners. The most successful combinations may be years in the making as plants are shifted around the garden and generally confused as to where and what their role is, and with whom. Meddling of this sort in the relationships of plants is necessary and frequent if gardeners aspire to glory in perennial bed design. However, satisfaction and reward are found at all levels of planting and arrangement, and gardeners who prefer to just jam-it-in-the-bed-and-watch-the-flowers-pop also find happiness.

After carefully studying admired groupings, gardeners can't fail to notice that these marriages frequently involve three partners, and perhaps the less said about that, the better. Suffice to point out that interest seems to hinge on an appreciable degree of complementary contrast in relationships of all kinds, and especially so in the garden, where features of form, color and texture are the main event. In basic terms this idea could be described as the desirable contrasts between bright and dull colors, finely cut and thickly broad shapes, smooth and fuzzy textures, vertical and horizontal forms.

The trick to putting successful associations together is to find plants with some element in common and one or more characteristics of contrast. Now it is apparent why this is not easy. Many plants could be found with obviously differing color and form, but finding a similar and shared feature is the challenge.

Consider the marriage of two familiar garden plants, hosta 'Krossa Regal' and Japanese painted fern (*Athyrium goeringianum* 'Pictum', zone 5). The hosta is tall and erect with thick, smooth leaves, veins of deeply incised straight lines and a suffusion of powdery gray over the leaf tissue. The Japanese painted fern is half the height of the hosta with finely cut fronds in a soft mounding form, and with a wash of gray across the lacy foliage. They are similar in color, but contrast in leaf texture and size makes a pleasing, if calm, association with just enough interest to merit attention. But adding a third plant, something to shake things up and make a bit of inspired mischief, could elevate this association to a more dynamic level worthy of a photograph.

Something bold needs to come into this marriage that is attractive to both partners individually, enhancing their shared and dissimilar values, and of course it must grow well in the same light and soil conditions. The catalyst in this grouping could be a third plant of striking color but smaller size. Perhaps an acceptable choice would be the deep purple leaves of the ground cover *Ajuga reptans* 'Braunherz' (zone 3), one of the darkest forms of bugleweed, with blue flower spikes in spring. Or possibly the bright golden-leaf form of creeping jenny (*Lysimachia nummularia* 'Aurea', zone 5), also blooming in spring with a carpet of lemony cup-shaped flowers.

Gardeners work for years trying to put these dynamic plant groupings together, sometimes finding the best matches happen spontaneously and by accident. Much time and mileage can be invested in tracking down just the right plant hybrids, and frequently what looks good, even brilliantly inspired, at the end of the day is not nearly so perfect in the light of the following morning. When the balance of contrast and similarity is just right and remains so in everyone's opinion for at least three days, that is an infrequently achieved moment of importance, on the level of cold fusion and nearly worth alerting the press. What is being made here is referred to in high-minded terms as aesthetic tension. As if there wasn't enough.

BRIDGING PLANTS

The average period of bloom for many perennial plants is less than three weeks, but some plant families continue to flower for up to six or eight weeks. By choosing selectively within a long-blooming family, it is possible to have flowers spanning the growing season and acting as a bridge through the brief periods when other plants are out of bloom. For instance, a backbone collection of three different cranesbill geraniums blooming early, mid-season and late will make a consistent base of floral display on which to build in other plants. Daylilies also can be acquired in early, mid-season and late-blooming selections and paired with one or two constantly blooming annual plants for a long show of color.

Plant families with long-blooming selections are black-eyed Susan (*Rudbeckia*), campanula, clematis, columbine (*Aquilegia*), coneflower (*Echinacea*), cranesbill geranium, daylily (*Hemerocallis*), meadow rue (*Thalictrum*), monkshood (*Aconitum*), phlox, roses, salvia, stonecrop (*Sedum*), yarrow (*Achillea*).

Toward succession bloom

"You should have seen it last week . . ." is the familiar lament of many a gardener with a wealth of May and June blossoms and leafy greenness the remainder of the summer. Along about August begins the season of despair, when burgeoning masses of flowers in multiple varieties are but a memory. Once again what was intended to be a sustained riot of bloom from spring into autumn has somehow dissipated with the shattering of the peonies. Orchestrating the successive blossoming of perennial plants from the earliest spring bloodroot (*Sanguinaria canadensis*, zone 3) to the latest autumnal Kamchatka bugbane (*Cimicifuga simplex*, zone 4) is more a matter of data collection than garden wizardry, requiring only an ability to take notes and use a calendar.

Each gardener will want to define what actually constitutes a "riot" in the garden. One little plant making a brave show of it in early April is something of a welcome curiosity, but three different plants all in bloom at that time seem a marvel of flowering and a reasonable standard of fullness. Three plants flowering simultaneously inspires the happy illusion that the garden is in business for the season. If one plant is in bloom, it is almost certain that two others can be found to bloom at the same time, and that is the immediate objective. Of course, any further plants that can be added to the minimum standard of three is gilding on the lily, and certainly constitutes a riot by any standard.

It will take approximately two growing seasons to get the garden into a display of continuous bloom from early spring to late autumn, but that is time well spent and with appreciable results all along the way. The American perennial gardener Frederick McGourty keeps a weekly journal, pursuing his own brand of religion every Sunday night by faith-

Expansive gardens offer opportunities to develop large beds with room for a community of many plants. But planting large spaces can be as perplexing as working with small ones. The keys are knowing what to plant for an extended season of bloom, and how many plants are required. Select at least three different varieties of perennial plants to bloom in each season: spring, early summer, late summer and autumn. Plant perennials in odd-numbered clusters of three or five of each variety to make thick clumps. Use spring bulbs, lilies and summer annuals to bridge gaps in perennial bloom. Bring a trellis or arbor into the bed for annual and perennial vines to climb. If the bed is long enough, colors can be organized with deep vivid tones at one end, blending toward cool pastels at the other end.

fully recording what is on display in the garden, even through the winter months. Gardeners of lesser acclaim but equal ambition can begin by making an inventory of plants in the garden and noting their flowering times on a calendar. The object is to fill in the blanks, researching plants that flower in the periods needed, and aiming for at least three different plant varieties blooming in each time period.

Experimentation is an exciting and necessary process in working toward sequential flowering times, and micro-climates within the garden can delay or accelerate the progress of each plant. This may result in the accumulation of plant material that does not perform exactly when planned, but that should be viewed only as a fortuitous excess.

Rely on memory as much as possible, using birthdays, annual picnics or any other events that can be associated with the memory of what was in bloom at a particular time. Then do some research to find plants that bloom when there is an obvious absence of flowers, and establish a budget for the season's purchases. Organizing information in this way immediately shows the gaps in the floral display and helps you to write a shopping list. If a friend or neighbor has something wonderful in bloom that you eagerly covet for a barren period, offer to trade for a piece of it. Bearing in mind that even the most circumspect gardener is a sensualist at heart, it is often more successful to offer an extravagant inducement, like wonderful cake or wine, to get what is desired.

Working with a chart on a single piece of paper, the growing season can be divided into three broad time segments, such as spring, summer and autumn. Or if more detail is desired, the segments can be increased to cover shorter periods in more detail. The average blossoming period for many perennials is fourteen to twenty-one days, and the segments can be structured to reflect this timing sequence. Filling out the chart will illustrate at a glance the periods of peak bloom in your garden, as well as the down-time in flower-power.

Keep them blooming

All any perennial plant wants is to make flowers that will age and turn into seed heads, ready to propagate the species. If spent blossoms are allowed to dry up and produce seeds, the plant will have completed its mission for the year and quickly shut down the blooming process to conserve energy. Yet the best-laid plans of a perennial plant can be thwarted by quick and clever gardeners with sharp shears. Cutting off flowers just as they are beginning to deteriorate, or deadheading, prevents seed formation. The plant will keep on pumping out flowers, trying to fulfill its mandate, and continued deadheading may lengthen the period of bloom by as much as two or three weeks.

Plant List

Use this chart to record the sequence of perennial bloom in your garden. List plants and check the time periods when they are in flower. Each box equals one week. Blank spaces will indicate the time periods when the garden is without flowers. Research plants that bloom in these periods and make a shopping list.

Plant	March	April	May	June	July	August	September	October	November

Southern blessings

Southern gardens are never entirely out of bloom, and many cool-weather perennial plants will contribute winter blossoms in warm regions.

Rock cress, *Arabis caucasica*, zone 5, full sun to part shade

Bloodroot, *Sanguinaria canadensis*, zone 3, full sun to part shade

Mazus, *Mazus japonicus*, zone 4, full sun to part shade

Hepatica, *Hepatica nobilis*, zone 5, part shade

Lenten rose, *Helleborus orientalis*, zone 4, full sun to part shade

Moss phlox, *Phlox subulata*, zone 3, full sun to part shade

Candytuft, *Iberis sempervirens*, zone 3, full sun

Sweet butterbur, *Petasites fragrans*, zone 5, full sun to part shade

Sweet violet, *Viola odorata*, zone 5, part shade

Adonis, *Adonis amurensis* and *A. vernalis*, zone 4, full sun

Late-blooming perennial plants, August to October

Autumn sunflower, *Helianthus rigidus* and *H. salicifolius*, zone 4, full sun

Boltonia, *Boltonia asteroides* 'Snowbank', zone 4, full sun to part shade

Cardinal flower, *Lobelia cardinalis*, zone 2, full sun to part shade

Hardy chrysanthemum, *Chrysanthemum* x *morifolium* hybrids, zone 5, full sun

Sweet autumn clematis (vine), *C. terniflora* or *C. paniculata*, zone 4, full sun

False sunflower, *Heliopsis helianthoides* hybrids, zone 4, full sun

Goldenrod hybrids, *Solidago rugosa* 'Fireworks' and 'Golden Fleece', zone 4, full sun

Japanese anemone, *Anemone* x *hybrida* hybrids, zone 6, full sun to part shade

Japanese toad lily, *Tricyrtis hirta* hybrids, zone 5, part shade to full shade

Joe-pye weed, *Eupatorium purpureum*, zone 3, full sun to part shade

Kamchatka bugbane, *Cimicifuga simplex*, zone 4, full sun to part shade

Michaelmas daisy, *Aster novi-belgii* hybrids, zone 4, full sun to part shade

Azure monkshood, *Aconitum carmichaelii*, zone 2, full sun to part shade

Obedient plant, *Physostegia virginiana* , zone 3, full sun to part shade

Sneezeweed, *Helenium autumnale* hybrids, zone 3, full sun

Showy stonecrop, *Sedum spectabile* hybrids, zone 3, full sun to part shade

Four

Trees, shrubs and vines

Living life large

Every city is built over a natural landscape that often was a forest, and for good reasons. Trees and woody plants grow where water is plentiful, and that is also a primary criterion for the growth of cities. After the earth has been cleared, covered with cement and asphalt, and all the holes and cracks carefully sealed to exclude light, moisture and oxygen, a few woody plants are put back as emblematic afterthoughts of the forest that once stood on the site. Vacant city lots left to their own devices will spontaneously return to meadows and finally to forests.

It is a sad fact that to acquire first-hand knowledge of the form, texture, blossoms and foliage of most indigenous woody plants, it is necessary to visit a park or arboretum, a kind of tree museum for living relics of the landscape. Most trees planted on city streets are the choices of bureaucrats, often monoculture plantings of imported trees, influenced by budget restraints and the frequency of maintenance required. It is a dismal picture, but not hopeless.

Trees are the largest living organisms on Earth, yet our awareness and regard of their presence and what they offer to human culture is casual at best. They are the living memory of a former era when trees never stood as solitary specimens on the edges of busy streets but were part of an arboreal community, a vast canopy of leaves and limbs stretching across the landscape.

Trees in cities are the primary processors of airborne pollutants, absorbing these gases and producing clean oxygen. They are the most dependable method for relief from summer heat, able to sustain cool micro-climates on the power of their own energy, and they provide protection from dangerous ultraviolet exposure. But most important, trees engage the imagination of those willing to allow large and important plants into the urban consciousness. Taking pleasure from their scale and character is a way of acknowledging the brief history of cities and people. With few exceptions, the physical stature and natural life span of most trees is greater and longer than that of humans.

People plant city trees for many reasons: to relieve the density of row housing, to punctuate the sprawl of commercial shopping malls, to create concealment, to make private a personal space. Some trees are planted to preserve a tradition of distant times and places; others are planted as a commitment to future generations. Certain ancient cultures surviving into modern times believe that trees hold spirits and can speak to those capable of hearing. It doesn't hurt to listen.

*Previous page: Suburban gardens provide a suitable venue for weeping willows (*Salix alba *'Tristis', zone 4), large trees with much sentimental association but seriously disruptive behavior when placed too close to city sewer systems. Sitting beneath the towering scaffold of willow branches fulfills the occasional emotional need to be lost in trees.*

Room to grow

Even the most beautiful tree can become a nuisance if it is too big for its space. Of course this is not the tree's fault but the consequence of the gardener's lack of information and foresight. Knowing the dimensions of the available space and the potential size of the tree to be planted are the prerequisites for a long and happy association. Measuring the site is easy enough, but understanding how tall and wide the tree will grow requires some interpretation.

The growth of all plants is affected by the climate and their hardiness zone rating. Temperature is the indicator that turns growth hormones on and off as seasons change and regulates the plant's growth. In warmer regions with longer growing seasons and higher winter temperatures, trees will achieve larger sizes. The fewer growing days and colder winters of cooler regions will retard the potential maximum growth of woody plants. Thus, a tree growing near the northern limit of its hardiness zone is less likely to achieve its full potential size, while the same tree growing several hardiness zones to the south will most likely be substantially larger.

A tree like white cedar (*Thuja occidentalis*, zone 2), sometimes referred to as *Eastern arborvitae*, has a very low hardiness zone and is capable of achieving its full potential of 60 feet (18 m) in height and 12 feet (3.5 m) in spread when grown in Maryland (zone 7); in a sheltered position, with excellent irrigation and fertilization, it could even reach 65 to 70 feet (19.5 to 21 m). But planted in Manitoba (zone 4), the shorter growing seasons, fewer days for manufacturing energy through photosynthesis, and severe winter conditions will limit the growth of the cedar, perhaps to 40 feet (12 m).

Other elements of climate have a role in regulating potential growth. Trees require significant quantities of water. A large maple will use several hundred gallons of water each day during the growing season, and it must all come from the soil. When grown in arid regions, trees are not able to carry out all the energy-making functions necessary to achieve potential growth, and they will be lower in structure and more sparsely foliated. Relentless wind has a similar effect, rapidly evaporating moisture from both the soil surface and the leaf tissue, causing foliage to dry out and interrupting the production of energy for growth.

Finally, light has an important role in growth, no matter what region the tree is grown in. The amazing ability of leaves to trap light energy and transform it into solid carbohydrate foods is the central factor in all plant growth. In insufficient light, leaves are unable to manufacture the full quotient of energy to achieve their potential growth. As a result, plants requiring full sun but grown in a shady garden will always be undersized, although they may still be big. However, some plants are genetically able to manufacture sufficient energy in low-light conditions, and they may well prosper and assume their maximum proportions.

Trees are often expensive to buy, heavy to move, difficult to plant and require several years of waiting before anything exciting happens. After all that, it is a crashing disappointment to find the wrong choice has been made. Far better to do the research, look at what is growing in the neighborhood, in parks and regional horticultural collections, and then make an informed decision that will give many years of satisfaction.

Gambling with hardiness zones

Trees planted near the edge of their hardiness zones may grow well for several years, but at some point can be expected to suffer damage from extremes of weather. An unusually cold winter can set back years of growth and disfigure the plant's natural form. Younger trees of smaller size will often have greater resilience after winter damage, and are more likely to adapt themselves to the challenging site.

By planting the tree near a brick wall and out of the wind, or on the warmer side of a group of large conifers, you can help make a micro-climate for the vulnerable tree, limiting the winter dieback, or dead wood, on twig tips and small branches. Some ornamental trees, such as the golden chain tree (*Laburnum x watereri* 'Vossii', zone 5), require protection from excessive cold during the first ten years, by which time they are sufficiently established to make strong growth with little damage even when at the northerly limit of their hardiness zone.

Gardeners who prefer not to gamble should plant trees that are two hardiness zones away from their northerly limits. Planting younger trees rather than larger, older ones will significantly increase successful wintering of the plants. Young trees root more effectively and grow rapidly, showing the results that will gratify the gardener's heart.

Small trees for city shade

Amur maple, *Acer ginnala*, zone 2, 15 to 25 feet (4.5 to 7.5 m)

Japanese maple, *Acer palmatum*, zone 5, 10 to 25 feet (3 to 7.5 m)

Downy serviceberry, *Amelanchier arborea*, zone 4, 15 to 25 feet (4.5 to 7.5 m)

Devil's walking stick, *Aralia spinosa*, zone 4, 10 to 20 feet (3 to 6 m)

White fringetree, *Chionanthus virginicus*, zone 3, 12 to 20 feet (3.5 to 6 m)

Pagoda dogwood, *Cornus alternifolia*, zone 3, 15 to 25 feet (4.5 to 7.5 m)

Kousa dogwood, *Cornus kousa*, zone 5, 10 to 20 feet (3 to 6 m)

Gray dogwood, *Cornus racemosa*, zone 4, 10 to 15 feet (3 to 4.5 m)

Cornelian cherry, *Cornus mas*, zone 4, 15 to 25 feet (4.5 to 7.5 m)

Spindle tree, *Euonymus europaeus*, zone 3, 12 to 25 feet (3.5 to 7.5 m)

Star magnolia, *Magnolia stellata*, zone 4, 10 to 20 feet (3 to 6 m)

American hophornbeam, *Ostrya virginiana*, zone 3, 20 to 35 feet (6 to 10.7 m)

Sourwood, *Oxydendrum arboreum*, zone 5, 15 to 30 feet (4.5 m to 9 m)

Persian parrotia, *Parrotia persica*, zone 4, 15 to 25 feet (4.5 to 7.5 m)

Mountain stewartia, *Stewartia ovata*, zone 5, 8 to 15 feet (2.4 to 4.5 m)

Japanese snowbell, *Styrax japonicus*, zone 5, 15 to 25 feet (4.5 to 7.5 m)

*As a backdrop to the rough-hewn stone bench, two special trees find appropriate space in a small urban corner.
The English oak (*Quercus robur *'Fastigiata', zone 5) and tri-color beech (*Fagus sylvatica *'Rosea-marginata',
zone 6, purple/pink/bronze leaves) bring strength and definition to a shady garden. The low light is sufficient
to keep both trees growing, but not so much that they outgrow their space.*

Trees for city gardens

Small trees do different things than big trees. They are closer, more accessible and can be appreciated in their entirety. We notice the full outline of their shape and demeanor and the fine points of each seasonal feature. Big trees are valued for their effect (providing shade, lowering temperature, creating mass and skyscape), but we are seldom familiar with their upper regions. Trees requiring minimal space bring architectural form into human scale. They fill the understory range between shrubs and sky-high plants, giving a sense of order, progression and completeness.

Among the many trees suitable for planting in small gardens, those with a fastigate (tall and narrow) shape are especially useful. These downsized hybrid cultivars of many familiar tall and wide-spreading trees can be used to frame a view or provide a focal point. They require minimal ground space for the root ball and cast little shade. Their tall, vertical form can be easily combined with shrubs and perennial plantings, and several trees can be set along a property line to provide structure or privacy without invasive growth on either side of the fence. In a contained or limited gardening space, they contribute style, dimension and interest without monopolizing the landscape.

Bear in mind that climate and the number of seasonal growing days control the height and spread of hardwood plants. Many trees do not reach their full potential growth in colder regions, which suits the small-space gardener very well. Conversely, growth may excel in gentler climates along the west coast and in warmer southern zones and achieve heights beyond expectation.

Newly installed shrubs and trees will show little, if any, growth in their first season, when they are establishing roots into the new

*Wasted space alongside a garage can be reclaimed for garden use. Removing the grass and installing an informal pathway keeps the space functional, but including a rustic arch and several interesting trees makes the most of this transitional area from front to back gardens. Weeping beech (*Fagus sylvatica *'Purpurea Pendula', zone 4) and fernleaf beech (*F. sylvatica *'Asplenifolia', zone 5) both hold their leaves in winter, providing four seasons of display along with the evergreen weeping Nootka false cypress (*Chamaecyparis nootkatensis *'Pendula', zone 5). The red Japanese maple (*Acer palmatum *spp., zone 5) is brilliant from spring into summer, along with Chinese flowering dogwoods (*Cornus kousa *var.* chinensis, zone 4) that display four weeks of white star-shaped blossoms in spring and red autumn berries. Purple blazing star (*Liatris spicata *'Kobold', zone 3) and white and yellow daylilies light up the path in late summer.*

*Small spaces can accommodate a small forest of specialty trees. The softly draping foliage of a chartreuse robinia tree (*Robinia pseudoacacia *'Frisia', zone 4) brings light to the shady entrance of a city garden. Dominating overhead are the wide-spreading branches and shaggy, apricot-brown bark of the dawn redwood (*Metasequoia glyptostroboides, *zone 5), a deciduous conifer with pyramidal form and soft, light green needles.*

planting hole. If consistent moisture is made available and root growth is successful, a flush of breaking new buds and tip growth will take place at the beginning of the second growing season, as roots continue to establish in the soil.

Generous twig and leaf growth can be expected from the third season onward. It takes approximately five years for woody plants to become established, that is, to grow into a mature form and to settle into a harmonious relationship with their companions and setting. After five years, well-cared-for plants will have adapted to the conditions of the site and have arranged their limbs to take full advantage of the available sunlight. They may have increased their size substantially since arrival and should be displaying good ornamental features.

Making an alley

Adapting classic design features to a small city garden creates a strong point of interest in a limited space. The idea of the alley is as old as Roman highways. Important boulevards were lined on each side with large trees, all of the same kind and dimension. Gardeners can make a similar statement with a row of tall, narrow trees to emphasize a walkway or frame a view in a small city garden. The trees should logically lead somewhere, perhaps from the street to a front door, or straight up the center of the garden to a bench or planted urn at the far end, with garden beds off to the side.

An alley can be made with any kind of narrow tree hybrid, but is particularly charming with ornamental fruit trees like callery pear or Siberian crabapple that are attractive in four seasons. The trees are smothered with blossom in spring, produce colorful ornamental fruit in summer that will not fall off, adopt bright colors in autumn and maintain strong architectural lines visible in winter.

When planting an alley, plan for the trees to be set 8 to 10 feet (2.4 to 3 m) apart so that they will not touch as they grow. The height

of the trees can be kept down to 12 to 15 feet (3.5 to 4.5 m) with annual pruning if desired, or they can be allowed to grow higher. The outline of each tree should be visible, and as years pass occasional side pruning may be necessary to maintain the profile of each tree.

Good trees for making an alley in a small garden are Japanese flowering cherry (*Prunus serrulata* 'Amanogawa', zone 5), callery pear (*Pyrus calleryana* 'Capital', zone 5) and European mountain ash (*Sorbus aucuparia* 'Aspleniifolia', zone 2).

Where space is limited, shrubs grafted

Tall and narrow trees for small spaces

Norway maple, *Acer platanoides* 'Columnare', zone 5, height 36 feet (11 m), spread 12 feet (3.5 m)
European white birch, *Betula pendula* 'Fastigiata', zone 2, height 33 feet (10 m), spread 6 feet (1.8 m)
Princeton sentry ginkgo, *Ginkgo biloba* 'Princeton Sentry', zone 4, height 36 feet (11 m), spread 12 feet (3.5 m)
Siberian crab apple, *Malus baccata* 'Columnaris', zone 2, height 24 feet (7 m), spread 6 feet (1.8 m)

Japanese flowering cherry, *Prunus serrulata* 'Amanogawa', zone 5, height 18 feet (5.5 m), spread 5 feet (1.5 m)
English oak, *Quercus robur* 'Fastigiata', zone 5, height 40 feet (12 m), spread 10 feet (3 m)
European mountain ash, *Sorbus aucuparia* 'Fastigiata', zone 4, height 30 feet (9 m), spread 6 feet (1.8 m)

Short and globe-shaped trees for small spaces

Norway maple, *Acer platanoides* 'Globosum', zone 4, height 12 feet (3.5 m), spread 15 feet (4.5 m)
Black locust, *Robinia pseudoacacia* 'Umbraculifera', zone 4, height 15 feet (4.5 m), spread 15 feet (4.5 m)
Little-leaf linden, *Tilia cordata* 'Green Globe', zone 4, height 15 feet (4.5 m), spread 6 feet (1.8 m)

Ornamental trees for small spaces

Apple serviceberry, *Amelanchier* x *grandiflora* 'Ballerina', zone 4, height 15 feet (4.5 m), spread 12 feet (3.5 m)
Weeping birch, *Betula pendula* 'Youngii', zone 2, height 15 feet (4.5 m), spread 10 feet (3 m)
Golden chain tree, *Laburnum* x *watereri* 'Vossii', zone 5, height 9 feet (2.7 m), spread 7 feet (2 m)
Lily magnolia, *Magnolia liliiflora* 'Susan', zone 4, height 8 feet (2.4 m), spread 8 feet (2.4 m)
Flowering crabapple, *Malus* 'Coralburst', zone 4, height 8 feet (2.4 m), spread 6 feet (1.8 m)

onto a standard-form trunk can be used in the same manner to form an avenue. Many shrubs are available in this style, and most are under 6 feet (1.8 m) in height. Winter-creeper (*Euonymus fortunei* 'Sarcoxie', zone 5), Meyer lilac (*Syringa meyeri* 'Palibin', zone 3) and Koreanspice viburnum (*Viburnum carlesii*, zone 4) are good choices for lining a pathway.

Splendor on the grass

The *tabula rasa* of a front lawn is an irresistible blankness to many gardeners with the urge to grow a tree. A plant that is to stand alone at center stage must have grace, style and distinguishing characteristics to carry off the spotlight effect through four seasons. Ideally its branching and foliage should have enough openness to allow one to partially see through the arboreal structure.

A tree that will stand for many years at the front of the garden must have a strong and universal appeal. Trees that consistently command admiration include almost any selection in the family of magnolias. Magnolias are a tree for all seasons, with a sensible symmetry to their structure, smooth grayness of bark and furry silver buds. A small but vocal contingent of detractors is critical of the effect of shattered magnolia blossoms on the lawn in the aftermath of blossoming time. To be fair, certain species with large petals, like the saucer magnolia (*Magnolia x soulangiana*,

zone 4) and the southern magnolia (*Magnolia grandiflora*, zone 7), do drop a multitude of petals, but they are so achingly beautiful as they drift onto the lawn that they justify any sweeping up necessary. Beyond this limited chore, the trees contribute a classical architecture with great style, seldom needing any pruning, and a foliage of strong substance and subtle luster. Several have a deep lemony fragrance capable of perfuming the entire garden in spring, and some rebloom sporadically in late summer.

Charming small-petaled cultivars make no litter, their petals simply curling up and disappearing into the lawn. Many species and hybrids are available in warm and cool regions. Potential size is also an adaptable feature, and various kinds are available for large and small settings. 'Goliath' is a cultivar of *Magnolia grandiflora* that produces creamy white flowers up to 12 inches (30 cm) across (expect to pick up the petals) on a reasonably compact plant, although still a big tree. Cultivars of the lily magnolia (*M. liliiflora*, zone 5) are altogether smaller but deliver substantial impact. The American woody plant authority Michael Dirr refers to this group as "The Little Girl Hybrids," and they include 'Ann', 'Betty', 'Jane', 'Judy', 'Pinkie', 'Randy', 'Ricki' and 'Susan', with blossoms in shades of pink and purple on shrubby plants small enough for postage-stamp lawns. With a mature height ranging between 8 and 15 feet (2.4 and 4.5 m), they are a valuable and rewarding asset in any garden.

An emblem of universal appeal, this 'Profusion' crabapple tree stands proudly unpruned and loaded with berries. With space to grow and assume its full form, the tree provides welcome shade from which to contemplate the vegetable patch beyond. Malus 'Profusion' is a crabapple with inbred resistance to apple diseases, and its foliage is clean and intact at the height of summer. Most of the berries are taken by birds and fallen fruit is never a problem.

Also worth noting among the medium-sized magnolias is 'Leonard Messel' (*Magnolia* x *loebneri* 'Leonard Messel', zone 5), growing to approximately 20 feet (6 m), with neat form and twelve-petal flowers flushed fuchsia pink on the backs and white inside (no pick-up from the lawn), and the smaller star magnolia (*Magnolia stellata*, zone 4), very slow growing to a height of 12 to 15 feet (3.5 to 4.5 m) and displaying the most silvery buds of its family and deepest lemon scent. All the magnolias like a cool, moist organic soil, and it is worth making careful preparation for them. They will grow well in light shade to full sun, but in bright light consistent moisture is crucial. When magnolias experience moisture stress, they will fail to set flower buds, and that is a sad event in any springtime.

Nobody's business

At the front of many small city gardens in older neighborhoods stand boulevard trees, planted by the municipal government in an effort to shade and grace the public sidewalk. Most are ignored, many are resented and few are loved, but their domination of the streetscape is complete.

There is no shortage of pejorative comment surrounding the placement of these trees: they make too much shade; grass will not grow under them; the leaf litter is voluminous; their invasive feeder roots strangle the life out of other plants and then find their way into the sewer system. It's not a happy situation.

Rather than give up on the front garden entirely, why not develop a little philosophy?

Further splendor on a small lawn

Several distinguished large trees are suitable to smaller settings. The two birch trees listed are both resistant to bronze birch borer, the modern plague of this lovely family.

River birch, *Betula nigra,* zone 4, height 30 feet (9 m), tan to pink bark
Asian White birch, *Betula platyphylla* var *japonica,* 'Whitespire' zone 5, height 30 feet (9 m), white bark
Deodar cedar, *Cedrus deodara,* zone 7, height 30 feet (9 m) in 20 years, conifer
Atlas cedar, *Cedrus atlantica,* zone 7, height 30 feet (9 m) in 20 years, conifer

Katsura tree, *Cercidiphyllum japonicum,* zone 4, height 40 feet (12 m)
Nootka false cypress, *Chamaecyparis nootkatensis* 'Pendula', zone 4, height 30 feet (9 m), weeping conifer
Fernleaved beech, *Fagus sylvatica* 'Asplenifolia', zone 5, height 40 feet (12 m)
Serbian spruce, *Picea omorika,* zone 5, height 40 feet (12 m), conifer
Colorado spruce, *Picea pungens* 'Fat Albert', zone 3, height 15 feet (4.5 m), conifer

Planting a tree

- Select a tree within your hardiness zone. Choose a location with sufficient light and soil that drains effectively. Be sure irrigation will be regularly available for the first two years after the tree is planted.
- Dig a saucer-shaped planting hole as deep as the root ball and twice as wide. Be sure the tree will sit about 1 or 2 inches (2.5 or 5 cm) above the surrounding soil. Replace up to a third of the soil from the hole with aged manure, peat moss and builder's sand.
- If the tree is in a fiberboard pot, remove the circular bottom with a sharp blade. Set the tree in the hole, surround it with some soil and use the blade to cut away the container sides. If the root ball is wrapped in burlap, put the tree in the hole and add some soil around it. Carefully unwrap the fabric, cutting away as much as possible and tucking the remainder down into the soil.
- Fill the hole three-quarters with soil and flood the hole with water to settle the soil. Allow the water to drain away, then fill in with the remaining soil. Firm the soil with your hands, but do not tread it down with your feet.
- Use some soil to form a rim around the root ball to catch and hold rainwater, and cover all exposed soil with 2 inches (5 cm) of an organic mulch.
- Pound stakes into the soil on each side of the tree just beyond the root ball. Slide a piece of soft hose over a length of heavy-gauge wire to protect the bark and loop the wire around the stake and the tree. Repeat on the other side of the tree.

If the tree is there to stay, making it the best it can be is the first step toward turning a debit into an asset. Use soil to form a saucer around the tree's base and water it regularly, allowing a hose to run slowly over the roots. Ask the municipal department responsible for boulevard trees in your area to prune it every 24 months, and request that minor branches be removed to allow light to penetrate and to increase air circulation. They will keep detailed records of the tree's condition and care, and will also make notes on the homeowner's comments and opinions. Let them know you intend to nurture the tree.

Rental trees

When you rent your premises, it is not always possible to plant a tree in the garden, but that is no reason to be treeless. Gardeners can have arboreal treasures close at hand by using large containers for young trees. This arrangement is not likely to satisfy the desire for a 60-foot (18 m) elm, but it will make trees a part of any gardener's day. A small tree placed by a front door or entry into the garden provides a welcome opportunity to see all its delicate details up close. Despite the diminutive size of the plant, its elevation in the box will make a stylish presentation and worthwhile garden feature.

Immature trees are adaptable to life in a box of premium soil with excellent drainage and adequate moisture and light. The container should be a minimum 36-inch (90 cm) cube, with many drainage holes drilled into the bottom. Spread a 4-inch (10 cm) layer of gravel in the bottom before you add the soil. In regions where frost is severe, a larger box gives better protection from frost, especially if it's lined with sheet Styrofoam. Be sure the plant is well within its hardiness zone limit. For instance, in southern New Jersey (zone 7), any tree with a hardiness rating of zone 5 or lower will winter well outdoors in a container. You can certainly try plants that are more tender, but consider it more of an experiment, since they may be lost in a cold snap. Trees in containers need to be carefully monitored, since containers can dry out rapidly in both warm and cold temperatures, particularly in windy locations. A mulch of manure in spring and autumn should be all the nutrients necessary.

If you move, the tree can go with you, providing the box can be lifted. Moving companies will take anything that fits into their truck. It's also possible to ask a local garden service to transport the box and tree. If the tree is to ride in the back of an open truck, cover the foliage with a sheet or plastic bag to prevent it from drying out.

Almost any kind of tree can be used if it is young enough that its root system fits comfortably in the container. Try Japanese tree lilac (*Syringa reticulata* 'Ivory Silk', zone 2), serviceberry (*Amelanchier canadensis*, zone 4), crabapple (*Malus*, zones 3 and 4), Eastern redbud (*Cercis canadensis*, zone 6), golden chain tree (*Laburnum* x *watereri* 'Vossii', zone 5), Japanese maple (*Acer palmatum*, zone 5), Shantung maple (*Acer truncatum*, zone 4), Amur maple (*Acer ginnala*, zone 2), cutleaf staghorn sumac (*Rhus typhina* 'Laciniata', zone 3), crape myrtle (*Lagerstroemia indica* zone 7), any form of small pine or cedar, and in frost-free regions any form of dwarf peach and citrus.

Shrubs

Easy elegance

Of the many kinds of plants city gardeners have to work with, shrubs are perhaps the most gratifying and versatile. Purchased as containerized plants, they arrive with a woody structure and are often capable of putting out foliage, flowers and sometimes fruits in short order. Even their somewhat diminutive arrival size is an advantage in projecting form and shape into empty spaces, and useful in the initial stages of setting up a garden when the slate is completely blank.

Old inherited shrubs are another matter. They have the benefit of mature form and wealth of blossom, but their dense structure and massive size can fill a lot of space. Renovating large shrubs by removing up to half of the oldest canes from the base can require a small pruning saw and strong arms. The result is a considerable improvement, revealing the plant's natural structure and allowing light and air to pass through. But to regain the square footage in a small garden, it may be necessary to entirely remove an old shrub.

Woody shrubs are the plant form of choice for establishing lines of definition in the garden. Their usefulness is almost endless for dividing and separating spaces and for creating form on the empty plane of a landscape. Several classical gardening techniques are based on the use of shrubby plants to form the complexities of Elizabethan knot gardens, French parterre gardens, mazes and displays of clipped topiary contrivance. The classic and ageless hedges of yew and boxwood are almost without parallel in providing a civilized containment to formal beds and borders, and a traditional cottage garden is founded on a structure of homely blossoming shrubs like quince, lilac, mock orange and rose of Sharon.

Shrubs come in all shapes, in regular and dwarf sizes, and some eventually grow into tree form, as many lilacs, yew and privet do. This occasionally comes as a surprise to the gardener, who may be getting more than was bargained for. All living things grow according to a complex genetic code, and each shrub has its own agenda. Gardeners might prefer to splice some genes and ghost-write the code themselves to get the desired results, but instead they must settle for intelligent choices and skillful pruning to keep growth under control. In city gardens where space is often at a premium, hard decisions may need to be made about any plant with a large floor plan. Shrubs take up valuable gardening area and must have enough ornamental features to justify their presence. A ten-day burst of yellow forsythia in spring may fill an entire corner of space and be quick rejuvenation for the color-starved soul, but what will it do for the garden over the following sixteen weeks of the growing season? Tough decisions are daily requirements when working with a small city garden.

Shrubs differ from trees in that they are low branching, with many trunks or a central crown sprouting many canes, and they generally grow up to only 15 feet (4.5 m) in height. Plants growing beyond that height are most often thought to be trees, although they may have a shrubby form. Many very large trees are also low branching, like the copper beech, and the casual distinctions between shrubs and trees are not hard and fast. Although shrubs can live for a long time and see generations of gardeners in and out of existence, trees have the edge on longevity and can live for many hundreds of years, some for thousands. As with all woody plants, climate and temperature zone strongly determine ultimate size: a butterfly bush (*Buddleia davidii*, zone 5) growing to a permanent height of 12 feet (3.5 m) in Georgia will be root hardy but die to the ground each winter in southern Ontario, only to resurrect itself every spring and grow to 4 feet (1.2 m). It's worth knowing that many shrubs are available in dwarf selections, and the Nanho series of butterfly bushes are more reasonably sized, 2 to 3 feet (60 to 90 cm) in the north and 3 to 5 feet (90 to 150 cm) in warmer zones.

Shrubs can provide privacy and security. They are useful for stopping the view of curious observers. Those plants with density and thorns can hold back the marauding crowds quite effectively. Many unsuccessful intruders bear the scars of encounters with the likes of fiveleaf aralia (*Acanthopanax sieboldianus*, zone 4) and shrub roses like 'Blanc Double de Coubert' or the 12-foot (3.5 m) climber 'Maigold'. Shrubs also serve to conceal what we don't want to see: garbage cans, compost bins, fire hydrants and air-conditioning units.

Perhaps most important is the special evolutionary place held by shrubs as the middle stage between the meadow and the forest, and the sustenance they provide to the diverse ecosystems that are dependent on their presence. Shrubs are plentiful producers of food and shelter for small animals and birds and a significant part of gardening heritage and cultural lore. Their persistence in the landscape gives context to the mythology of "hedgerow" literature, such as *The Wind in the Willows*, which continues to charm generations of child naturalists. Shrubs embody all that is desirable in a plant: the form, foliage, flower and fruits of each season, and the romantic and sentimental associations of texture and scent. Shrubs are the real deal in gardening.

Urban problems

City gardens often have more than one kind of site condition to cope with, reflecting the diverse assortment of trees and structures surrounding them. Dry soil conditions, in both

*Large forest trees in a small city garden are useful backdrops for a stream, pond and dwarf weeping birch (*Betula pendula *'Youngii', zone 2). Big evergreen trees are assets when appropriately placed in far corners, filling the sky with form and providing a sense of enclosure, privacy and maturity. In older gardens hemlock and spruce are often inherited, but new gardens can be planted with similar trees that will grow quickly. Eastern white pine (*Pinus strobus, *zone 3, height 60 feet/18 m), pyramid cedar (*Thuja occidentalis *'Fastigata', zone 3, height 50 feet/15 m) and Canadian hemlock (*Tsuga canadensis, *zone 4, height 65 feet/20 m) are suitable choices for dramatic city skyscapes.*

sun and shade, result when buildings cover the soil and divert rainwater into sewer systems, and massive volunteers (that is, self-seeded mature trees) spread their roots and consume the moisture supply. These circumstances call for serious gardening decisions.

Coping with challenges of soil, light and moisture is considerably simplified when you choose shrubs with the right genetic fortitude. Characteristics drawn from distant gene pools in each shrub's heritage can make a big impact in the successful planting of problem areas. Ethnobotanists make careers of tracing the historical sources of plant characteristics, but gardeners are satisfied to discover what works well in the garden and run with it.

Dry shade is possibly the most common and challenging city garden circumstance. The double deprivation of low light and inadequate moisture leaves plants in considerable jeopardy, with few resources for manufacturing carbohydrate energy. Shrubs in these con-

Shrubs for dry shade

Fiveleaf aralia, *Acanthopanax sieboldianus*, zone 4
False spirea, *Sorbaria sorbifolia*, zone 2
Amur honeysuckle, *Lonicera maackii*, zone 2
Wayfaring tree, *Viburnum lantana*, zone 3
Nannyberry, *Viburnum lentago*, zone 2

Snowberry, *Symphoricarpos albus*, zone 3
Gray dogwood, *Cornus racemosa*, zone 4
Black jetbead, *Rhodotypos scandens*, zone 4
Flowering raspberry, *Rubus odoratus*, zone 4

Shrubs for dry, sunny sites

Smoke tree, *Cotinus coggygria* 'Royal Purple', zone 5
Siberian peashrub, *Caragana arborescens* 'Lobergii', zone 2
Cranberry cotoneaster, *Cotoneaster apiculatus*, zone 4
Devil's-walkingstick, *Aralia spinosa*, zone 5
Cardinal autumn olive, *Elaeagnus umbellata* 'Cardinal', zone 5

Russian olive, *Elaeagnus angustifolia*, zone 2
Bottlebrush buckeye, *Aesculus parviflora*, zone 3
Beauty bush, *Kolkwitzia amabilis*, zone 4
Ninebark, *Physocarpus opulifolius* 'Dart's Gold', zone 2
Fragrant sumac, *Rhus aromatica* 'Gro-low', zone 4

Shrubs for chronically wet soil

Serviceberry, *Amelanchier canadensis*, zone 4
Summersweet, *Clethra alnifolia* 'Paniculata', zone 4
Silverleaf dogwood, *Cornus alba* 'Elegantissima', zone 2
Yellowtwig dogwood, *Cornus stolonifera* 'Flaviramea', zone 2
Slender deutzia, *Deutzia gracilis*, zone 5

Witch hazel, *Hamamelis virginiana*, zone 5
Winterberry, *Ilex verticillata*, zone 4, male and female necessary
Blue arctic willow, *Salix purpurea* 'Nana', zone 4
Chenault coralberry, *Symphoricarpos* x *chenaultii* 'Hancock', zone 5

ditions grow tall and straggly as they search for water and light to fill out their bare branches. Eventually the twigs begin to die back as the roots are unable to provide the necessities of life. Dry soil in bright light also jeopardizes shrub growth by supplying too little of one necessity and too much of the other. With insufficient water, plant tissues sizzle in all-day sun and eventually become desiccated and unable to manufacture carbohydrates.

Less frequent but still a bothersome situation are gardens with excessive accumulations of moisture. These are the thoughtless blunders of builders wanting to take advantage of every scrap of land without going to the expense of correcting the grading, and with little regard for the large drainage problems they create. But choosing shrubs with a genetic ability to adapt to these conditions makes for inspired planting and a sense that some things can be made right in this world.

Drawing lines

Many shrubs planted in lines, shoulder-to-shoulder, are of course a hedge, although it is not necessary for them to be identical in kind or uniform in habit. Plants used this way make the gardener's most forceful statement about ownership, use of space and definition of purpose.

Hedges have been used since Roman times to mark the boundary of a garden, and the method is still practiced in city gardens and along country roads. A hedge is infinitely dynamic as a boundary marking, offering many design values, an option to prune to various heights, and diverse aesthetic components through four seasons. A hedge can be relatively unchanging, or it can be chosen for its variable features and changeability.

Using a hedge along the lot line between city gardens is a gracious way to mark the territory and ensure some privacy, but it can be a nuisance if the plants are not well chosen or the hedge isn't maintained. Many ratty and miserable hedges are to be seen, planted and forgotten, or inherited in the move from one city garden to another. Our appreciation of hedges is dulled by so many poor examples, but a well-maintained hedge is truly a thing of beauty. A silk purse can often be made from a sow's ear by renovating an old inherited hedge and restoring it to its former glory.

When planting a new hedge, the choice of plant is of primary importance. The plant must be suited to the available light and moisture conditions and should require minimal care. Most gardeners want a vigorous hedge that will fill in quickly, then stay still for the rest of the century. This is not a likely scenario. Every hedge will require moisture and nourishment and a once-a-year assessment of growth and trimming needs. And a vigorous plant will continue to express its energy in predictable directions, mostly up and outward. It is far better to choose a slower-growing plant that can be easily contained at the desired height with a little trimming after its

Where space is limited, a low evergreen hedge of boxwood or yew is the classic choice to define a boundary. Shearing plants into precise shapes requires careful and frequent trimming to maintain their form. The shaped plants provide an architectural contrast against a relaxed background of neighboring trees and focus attention on the stone terrace.

spring growth period. Or better yet, use dwarf plants with a genetically limited pattern of growth near to the height desired. These dwarfs are not really so small. They make excellent divisions between gardens and can be allowed to assume their full growth and form.

Even though your intention is to mark boundaries, planting a hedge directly on the property line can tempt the judgment of Solomon. Haggles over ownership and treatment of the plants can sour the relationship between neighbors. If the neighboring property is sold, the newcomers will presume they own at least the half of the hedge on their side of the line and may have ideas and methods of their own to deal with it. Unless your garden borders on a cemetery, whence the comment is usually low key, it's best to plant at least 24 inches (60 cm) inside the lot line. If new neighbors go so far as to put up a fence, at least most of the hedge will be uninjured.

Planting a low ornamental hedge at streetside where the lawn meets the sidewalk is useful to indicate private property, but first check your municipal bylaws to be sure this is allowed. The first foot or two of lawn is in the no-man's-land between public and private and is often subject to the abuses of people and animals. Municipal property usually extends from the boulevard and can take in up to a third of the lawn area, but it is assumed the owner will garden and tend this bit of real estate as if it were private.

Where bylaws prohibit a hedge on city property, the easiest solution is to plant the hedge just at the point where city property ends and private property begins. There is a tendency for the front lawn to flow visually into the sidewalk, losing its sense of identity with the house, and a low hedge, 3 to 5 feet (90 to 150 cm) in height, is an effective design strategy to enclose and hold back this private space. Low hedges are usually best in front of houses, since they allow a good sight line over the hedge (a security consideration) and won't obstruct visibility when you're backing out of the driveway.

BARE ANKLES

The base of a hedge should not be allowed to fill up with weeds. To prevent lawn mower injuries to the branches, and also to limit the competition for moisture, turf grass should be stopped with a sharp edge and prevented from covering the soil under hedge branches. Spread an organic mulch of shredded bark or leaves over the roots and under the branches. The mulch will conserve soil moisture and slowly degrade into nutrients.

It is also possible to cover a hedge's ankles with an ornamental ground cover. Select a carpeting form of plant that will not give too

Spreading cheer

There is no more jolly sight in early spring than exuberant bursts of bright crocus all along the feet of a hedge. This is a wonderful display to begin the growing season, and a good show before herbaceous groundcover plants make their appearance. As the ground cover grows it will help to hide the fading crocus foliage.

*Inheriting an old hedge is an opportunity to rehabilitate a once-proud planting. This hedge of American horn-beam (*Carpinus americana, *zone 3) has withstood the abuses of a busy urban corner for many decades, and the current gardener has carefully shaped it and provides regular irrigation. Mulch over the roots keeps moisture in the soil and a planting of violas helps to distract from the bare ankles. Native American hornbeam is attractive and useful as a hedge or tree, with potential growth to 20 or 30 feet in part to full sun. It is tolerant of wet soils and will withstand seasonal flooding. Autumn color is a combined yellow, orange and scarlet.*

much root competition. For any light level the tiny 'Kewensis' euonymus (*Euonymus fortunei* 'Kewensis,' zone 5) is an effective and charming choice. In shady locations two good choices are sweet woodruff (*Galium odoratum,* zone 5) and English ivy (*Hedera helix,* zone 5), although the ivy may be too vigorous in warmer regions. In brighter light any of the spotted dead nettles (*Lamium maculatum,* zone 4) are an attractive covering, particularly 'White Nancy', with bright blossoms and foliage.

PROVIDING RELIEF

An uneven and scruffy appearance to a hedge, with many bare branches and holes in the sides, is often caused by inadequate moisture and nutrients. It is worth remembering that these large woody plants grow in close quarters, with quite a bit of competition for the necessities of life, and they require as much thoughtful attention as any other planting.

The most effective way to water a hedge is to lay a soaker or weeper hose at the feet for the season and turn it on regularly. Woody shrubs require a deep watering approximately every ten days, and will benefit from a generous feeding of compost or aged manure once a year, in spring or autumn.

Holes in hedges can also be the result of winter ice damage. Light snow is no problem to a hedge and makes a pretty winter picture. But an accumulation of heavy snow can partially melt and turn into ice, burning evergreen foliage and breaking thin twigs and branches. When snowfall is heavy, use a broom to brush off major accumulations before they turn into ice.

HARD FACTS ABOUT SHEARING

Shearing is a radical thing to do to a hedge or shrub, but for centuries gardeners have cut all surfaces of hedges to one uniform plane, usually in geometric shapes like rectangles or cubes, or other ornamental representations mimicking small animals and teapots. This radical trimming causes the shrub to activate buds in an effort to regain its form, and then the shearing must be done again. A hedge kept in rigidly sheared condition will require this attention at least three times in the growing season. Hedges that are closely clipped will defoliate at the bottom if the top branches are

Plants for top-sheared hedges

Alpine currant, *Ribes alpinum*, zone 2, height 2 to 5 feet (60 to 150 cm)
European beech, *Fagus sylvatica*, zone 4, height up to 10 feet (3 m)
Purple beech, *Fagus sylvatica* 'Riversii', zone 4, height up to 10 feet (3 m)
Boxwood, *Buxus*, zone 5, height 1 to 3 feet (30 to 90 cm)
White cedar, *Thuja occidentalis*, zone 2, height up to 10 feet (3 m)
Peking cotoneaster, *Cotoneaster acutifolius*, zone 2, height 3 to 5 feet (90 to 150 cm)

Wintercreeper euonymus, *Euonymus fortunei* 'Sarcoxie', zone 5, height 2 to 4 feet (60 to 120 cm)
Canadian hemlock, *Tsuga canadensis*, zone 4, height up to 10 feet (3 m)
San Jose holly, *Ilex* x *aquipernyi* 'San Jose', zone 6, height up to 10 feet (3 m)
Amur privet, *Ligustrum amurense*, zone 5, height 4 to 8 feet (1.2 to 2.4 m)
Hicks's yew, *Taxus* x *media* 'Hicksii', zone 5, height 5 to 10 feet (1.5 to 3 m)

Plants for low hedges
(under 5 feet (1.5 m) in height)

Alpine currant, *Ribes alpinum*, zone 2, sun or shade
'Mint Julep' juniper, *Juniperus* x *media* 'Mint Julep', zone 4, sun
Hicks's yew, *Taxus* x *media* 'Hicksii', zone 5, sun or shade, berries are poisonous
Dwarf burning bush, *Euonymus alatus* 'Compactus', zone 3, sun
Dwarf Korean lilac, *Syringa meyeri* 'Palibin', zone 3, sun to part shade
Boxwood, *Buxus microphylla*, zone 5, sun to shade

Many roses can be used as hedges, and one that gives consistent performance and blooms until frost is the floribunda rose 'Nearly Wild', growing to a height of 3 to 4 feet (90 to 120 cm) and very winter-hardy. A single rose with slight scent, it forms enough mass to qualify as a hedge plant and has medium pink petals with prominent golden anthers. This rose has little winter value but is suitable for hedging around a patio or along a garden path.

wider and shade the lower branches. The appropriate form is broader at the base and narrower toward the top, allowing sunlight to fall on the full surface of the sides.

Shearing has a weakening effect on a hedge. Repeated cutting causes all the new growth to form in a thin outer layer, leaving the interior branches bare. This reduction in total leaf surface decreases the tissue available for photosynthesis, and the shrubs are unable to manufacture sufficient carbohydrate energy. Winter injury from ice and snow eventually causes some patchy losses of foliage. Not always a pretty picture

BUT IF YOU INSIST

Despite all advice to the contrary, you may decide to shear a hedge. You will require a focused attitude and steady hand. Set up a guideline with stakes and string and use a spirit level to be sure the top line is straight. Work slowly and step back for an assessment every 6 feet (1.8 m) to be sure the work is headed in the right direction. The finished width of the bottom should always be wider than the top. If possible, use long hand shears for this work. The electric hedge trimmer has all the subtlety of a chain saw and can make hash of a hedge with one small slip of the hand.

Very old hedges may not respond well to heavy pruning. Old flowering hedges in a sunny location may generate new growth. However, if trees that were young when the hedge was planted are now mature and blocking sunlight, a new hedge of shade-tolerant plants may be required. Old evergreen plants such as yew, cedar and juniper will not sprout from bare interior wood, and they are best replaced with a new hedge.

A SALTY DIET

Hedges along a sidewalk are likely to get a good dose of winter road salt in cold regions. Salt has a doubly injurious effect, burning the foliage of coniferous evergreens in winter and collecting in the soil, where it will be absorbed by roots in spring. Stakes with burlap fabric are sometimes erected as a screen on the street side of the hedge, but this is a poor barrier: when it's saturated, the salt-laden burlap will press against the foliage. Instead, use thick plastic sheeting stapled to the stakes and extending 10 inches (23 cm) above the top of the hedge. The stakes and sheeting should be placed so there is only minimal contact with the plants.

SPACING

When setting the spacing for a hedge, much depends on the kind of plants chosen. The rule of thumb is approximately 18 to 24 inches (45 to 60 cm) between centers (meaning main trunks or crowns) for a hedge that will grow together, with no profiles of individual plants. This spacing is suitable for a hedge of cedar or boxwood that will mass together and be clipped to a consistent height. If plants are to retain their individual profiles and form, as with dwarf juniper or dwarf lilac, allow sufficient room for them to develop: 3 to 4 feet (90 to 120 cm) between centers is necessary.

Planting a bare-root rose

Dormant bare-root roses are kept in cold storage until shipping time in late autumn or early spring. The advantage in ordering bare-root roses by mail is that they are put into the soil well ahead of the growing season and will have an early start on root development. Planting into cold soil allows root growth without stimulating shoots and leaves.

When the roses arrive, open the package immediately to check for signs of fungus. A small section of fungus can be brushed away and the area dusted with powdered sulfur. If serious fungus or mold infection is present, return the plants to where you bought them. If planting is delayed a day or two, leave the roses in their package, but they must be planted by the third or fourth day.

- Examine the roots and cut off any wispy root ends, leaving a sturdy bundle no more than 12 inches (30 cm) long. The canes have been pruned at the nursery and don't require any further cutting. Prepare a hole deep and wide enough to comfortably accommodate the roots, with the bulging graft union (where the plant is grafted onto the rootstock) 1 to 2 inches (2.5 to 5 cm) below soil level.

- Set the roots into the hole and fill three-quarters with soil that has been generously amended with compost or aged manure and 1 cup of bone meal. Flood the hole with water and allow it to drain, then fill the rest of the hole with soil. Tamp down the soil with your hands only. Treading with your feet will drive oxygen out of the soil and compact the roots.

- Don't use any fertilizers other than compost and aged manure at this time. Strong fertilizers can be given after June, when the plant is in full leaf.

Large shrubs in small spaces

There is great joy to be had from flowering shrubs, but it is often short lived. Many of the shrubs associated with blossoms and scent, like flowering quince and lilac, produce seasonal display that is long anticipated but short in duration. After two or at most three weeks of bloom, the green scaffolding is all that is left for the rest of the gardening season.

When pride of place in a small city garden is given over to a large flowering shrub with important, if brief, ornamental value, it helps to bring something more into the picture. The shrub can remain the central event, but carefully chosen companions adaptable to tight quarters can help to make better use of the space. For example, at the foot of a French hybrid lilac in a sunny location, you might plant earliest-blooming snowdrops and low-growing tulips, flowers that will bloom before the shrub's foliage is apparent. This display

A diminutive front garden can make a big impression when it's packed with plants instead of grass. The wide archway is a friendly gesture placed close to the sidewalk and supports a hedgerow community of climbing roses, clematis and billowing perennials with masses of honeysuckle against the porch.

could be followed by later-blooming daffodils to coincide with the flowering of the lilac, and then a colorful planting of hybrid tetraploid daylilies (three plants, all the same hybrid) to hide the ripening foliage of the bulbs and provide four weeks of bloom from June to the end of July. Finally, a late-blooming clematis can be planted alongside the lilac and allowed to wander through the shrub, producing its blossoms wherever it wants in August.

This is just one of many possible schemes. The important criterion in plant selection is available light. Everything must be happy to perform in whatever light is available. In bright light the bulbs' foliage will generate enough energy to bloom the following year. But in low light it is easier to plant fresh bulbs each year as light is probably insufficient to make another year's blossom. Not many bulbs are required to make a good showing, and this should not be an unreasonable expense.

The city hedgerow

Some pleasures of the country garden are easily transportable to the city, and one of them is the hedgerow, or mixed shrub border. Where space allows, perhaps along the side of a long driveway or bordering one side of a garden, a selection of shrubs chosen for a staggered succession of bloom complements the changing of the seasons in a small garden landscape. This is low-maintenance, high-satisfaction gardening at its best, for the border requires only occasional attention and rewards the gardener with diversity in blossom, scent and form.

The border can be any size and dimension, using either full-size or dwarf shrubs. The "bones" of the hedgerow must have strong winter value and vertical form, and many kinds of evergreens are suitable. These structural plants will need to be in scale with the site, and a small shrub border could be anchored by two or three slow-growing dwarf Alberta spruce (*Picea glauca* var. *albertiana* 'Conica', zone 4); a larger border could accommodate several emerald cedars or 'Wichita Blue' junipers (*Juniperus scopulorum* 'Wichita Blue', zone 4). These structural plants are meant to give the border substance and anchor it in the landscape, and they should have clear, simple lines to display the features of the blossoming shrubs around them.

This border offers an opportunity to display a collection of your favorite shrubs, although you should try to select a span of plants that blossom from earliest spring through autumn. The season might begin with a collection of daphnes, including the earliest rosy-purple February daphne (*Daphne mezereum*, zone 5), low-growing rose daphne (*D. cneorum*, zone 4) with bright rosy-pink blooms in April, and followed by the lovely variegated daphne 'Carol Mackie' (*D.* x *burkwoodii*, zone 4) blossoming in May. The daphnes are a gardener's winter dream come true, highly scented and very early flowering with small enough form to fit most places. They perform well in light shade to sun, and carry highly ornamental berries in early summer with charming, delicate foliage. The berries, however, are poisonous.

The progression of blossom can include forsythia, flowering quince, the early scented Koreanspice viburnum (*Viburnum carlesii*, zone 4) and fragrant snowball viburnum (*V.* x *carlcephalum*, zone 5), lilac, deutzia, spirea, weigela, shrub roses, mock orange, beautybush, hydrangea, rose of Sharon, witch hazel and highbush cranberry (*Viburnum trilobum*, zone 2) with bright red berries at the end of summer. Many other choices exist and most large shrubs come in dwarf sizes, and often with more than one flower color. It is possible to mix full-size shrubs with dwarf forms in front.

A collection of woody plants will benefit from a bit of variation in color and texture. Many flowering shrubs can be had with variegated green-and-cream leaves, such as variegated weigela, which combines the light quality of its leaves with pink-and-white blossoms, making a frilly spot in the border. Plants with yellow leaves, such as golden mock orange (*Philadelphus coronarius* 'Aureus', zone 4) and goldmound spirea (*Spiraea* x 'Gold Mound', zone 4), will also brighten the border whereas dark leaves like purpleleaf sand cherry (*Prunus* x *cistena*, zone 3) will make areas of contrast. Ornamental grasses are perhaps worth including for their strong texture and form, particularly in the last part of the growing season when they flower with silky and generous tassels.

Removing a large woody shrub

Removing the upper structure of a woody plant is a straightforward procedure. But the business end of the project is underground, where roots have made a stronghold in the soil for many years. To avoid breaking expensive shovels and tender tempers, don't work against the roots. Work around them.

The two keys to digging out a large shrub or small tree are sharp tools, and using the structure of the plant to help in its removal. Blunt-nosed spades, long-handled shovels, short hatchets, lopers and tree saws should be sharpened each spring. You can use a mill file purchased from a hardware store, carefully stroking the file across the metal cutting edge of the blade, always in one direction and not back and forth. A service that sharpens lawn mowers will also do an expert job on garden tools.

- Cut the plant down in pieces, using hand pruners, lopers and a tree saw to remove branches and sections of trunk. Leave standing a section of the central trunk or woody scaffolding about 24 to 36 inches (60 to 90 cm) in height. This will be useful for rocking and levering the plant out of the ground if the root system is reluctant to let go.

- Starting close to the main crown or trunk, use the shovel to dig soil away from the roots. As the structure of the roots is exposed, begin to loosen them in the earth by grasping the branches and rocking the plant back and forth. Continue digging soil away from the root structure and follow it as far as possible, stopping periodically to loosen the roots by rocking. Soon you will identify the areas of the root system that are holding tight.

- Use the sharp edge of the blunt-nosed spade to thrust through fibrous feeder roots and thin woody roots, and continue to agitate larger sections by rocking. When you have cut all the easier woody sections, use the hatchet or the saw to cut through thicker roots that are resisting removal.

- It is not necessary to remove every bit of root, but try to get everything in the top 12 inches (30 cm) of soil. Most shrubs and trees that regenerate stems and suckers require the crown of the plant to be left intact. Removing the root system to a foot below soil level should eliminate the crown and potential regrowth.

Forsythia monsters

The twentieth century will be remembered as a time when only one selection of forsythia was commonly acknowledged, and that was the monster kind. They still exist and will live on forever as 10-foot (3 m) specimens in forgotten corners where gardeners have given up, and not even annual leveling with a machete will keep them down.

Forsythia is a wonderful shrub and so inseparable from the idea of spring that the season could not happen without it. Forsythia lovers will always buy this plant before any other, often unwittingly purchasing the 10-foot (3 m) variety and installing it prominently at the front of the border, where it assumes prairie-silo proportions.

The good news is that a broad selection of heights is available in the forsythia department of better plant nurseries, and it is worth seeking out the appropriate size for small city gardens. Forsythia is a plant that spreads much joy and rivals only the infamous willows in vigor and exuberance. Its missionary zeal needs only a bit of genetic manipulation to keep within the bounds of city limits.

Pruning forsythia

Meddle with forsythia and you take on a force of nature. The best strategy is to plant the size of forsythia most suitable to the space and let the shrub assume its natural proportions. If you have inherited a shrub that is too big for

Forsythias: Getting a grip on size

Dwarf greenstem forsythia (*Forsythia viridissima* 'Bronxensis', zone 5) grows to 18 inches (45 cm) in height with a flat-topped mounded form, green stems and yellow flowers, and can be used as a low hedge for bordering walkways.

'Happy Centennial' forsythia (*F.* x *ovata* 'Happy Centennial', zone 5) grows to a height of 2 to 3 feet (60 to 90 cm) and a spread of 3 to 5 feet (90 to 150 cm), with fragrant flowers.

'Arnold Dwarf' forsythia (*F.* x *intermedia* x *F. japonica* 'Arnold Dwarf', zone 5) grows to 3 feet (90 cm) in height and can be used as a low-spreading ground cover.

Weeping forsythia (*F. suspensa*, zone 6) grows to 4 feet high (1.2 m), with fountain-like cascading canes that spread to 6 feet (1.8 m). Excellent for use as ground cover on an embankment or for trailing over walls. Bright yellow flowers in spring.

'Ottawa' early forsythia (*F. ovata* 'Ottawa', zone 4) grows to 5 feet (1.5 m), is hardier than other forsythias and blooms two weeks earlier.

'Northern Gold' forsythia (*F.* 'Northern Gold', zone 3) has greater cold hardiness than other selections and an upright form that grows to 6 feet (1.8 m).

'Lynwood Gold' forsythia (*F.* x *intermedia* 'Lynwood Gold', zone 4) is a large plant with big golden blossoms in upright form reaching 8 feet (2.4 m).

Showy border forsythia (*F.* x *intermedia* 'Spectabilis', zone 6) reaches a monstrous height of 10 to 12 feet (3 to 3.5 m) with equal width, forming a dense thicket of canes.

your small city garden, dig it out and replace it with a more appropriate size.

If you must prune a forsythia, it's best to understand how the shrub will react. Forsythia is a vigorous plant, especially when grown in a sunny location. Pruning canes back triggers the growth of buds just behind the point of the cut, and they will quickly sprout numerous buds to make up for the loss in cane length. This reaction results in a thicker shrub returning to the original height. The forsythia is still too big and there is more of it.

A compromise can be reached by allowing the plant to keep its natural height but thinning the number of canes from the base. This will make an attractive arching shrub that you can see through. It will still be big, but it will have a graceful and more delicate appearance.

Forsythia blooms on twigs that grow from the main structural canes. The twigs grow in the first season and bloom in the second spring. Prune forsythia immediately after it finishes blooming. When thinning canes from the base, remove the wood that bloomed in the current year, and be sure to leave the canes that will carry flowers next spring.

Vines

Rampant in the garden

Gardening encompasses a strange mix of appreciations and inhibitions. The appeal of plants with jungle naturalism and sometimes extravagant bloom is tempered by a sense of apprehension when the object of desire takes off on its own road. Vines are outlaw plants, loved for their lush character and feared for their errant ways. They are an intriguing mix of elegant form and primitive instinct to roam the earth. Many associations exist between these climbing plants and social history. The extraordinary hanging flower panicles of wisteria, some a full 36 inches (90cm) of elegant cascade, are a classic insignia of Japanese culture spanning many centuries. Other vines, such as the "woodbine," or sweetly scented honeysuckle, are referred to throughout Shakespearean literature. The classic 'Heavenly Blue' morning glory is emblematic of small cottage gardens with white picket fences, and English ivy is traditionally associ-

*The classic combination of New Dawn rose and Jackmanii clematis are espaliered on a brick wall, part of a demolished garage left standing and adapted as a garden room. Now open to the sky and framed in with heavy beams above, the garage provides space for dining among perennial plants. Many clematis climb posts and the wall, and oakleaf hydrangea (*Hydrangea quercifolia, *zone 5) fills the corners in company with perennial geraniums, primulas and lenten rose (*Helleborus orientalis, *zone 5). Just beyond the door frame are a row of English oaks (*Quercus robur *'Fastigiata', zone 5) and roses lining the path.*

ated with "ivy league" universities and vine-covered halls.

In small city gardens, vines offer great opportunities for vertical growing and can strongly influence the spirit of the place. Their "footprint" is limited, requiring only a few square feet to get into the ground, but the aerial possibilities are awesome. There are vines for every circumstance, and the primary criteria for selection is the right support for their climbing needs and appropriate spaces for them to wander. Most vines have one or more methods of gaining elevation, such as tendrils, sticky disks or twining movement, although they are amazingly adaptive and may switch methods to cover more territory. Some vines require no assistance and will roll up and over on their own energy (sometimes a mixed blessing), without benefit of climbing devices. Vines with this ability have an arcing and pulsing action, and their form and energy can be seen in the movements of pumpkin vines as they mount an unattended garden shed to set their fruit on the roof.

Window panes

No gardener wants to crawl through a tiny cramped space, and neither does any plant. The open spaces in a trellis, referred to as window panes, should be as generous as possible to allow the easy passage of twining vines. Window panes 2 inches (5 cm) square are just barely adequate. Generally larger is better. Vines can find their way through the smallest opening, but will not appear graceful in transit, and the point is for the relationship between trellis and plant to appear natural and relaxed.

Vines are clever opportunists, able to find the tiniest opening and insinuate themselves through to the other side. Wisterias develop great physical strength in their maturity and are capable of lifting a roof, appearing suddenly in the bedroom to the midnight delight or dismay of dreamers. Grape vines possess extraordinary vigor and will push through the corner of a screened window. Bystanders to the event view these intrusions as clear indicators that nature is shockingly in the ascendancy, but gardeners are excited and gratified by the melding of interior and natural worlds.

Twixt the trellis and the wall

Walls of brick, stucco and wood board absorb and radiate heat and make an encouraging micro-climate for vine growth. The trick to making a vine comfortable and at ease on a wall-mounted trellis is to allow sufficient room for the tendrils and canes to slip under. Small vines require 2 inches (5 cm) of space to pass between the wall and trellis without appearing as if they are trying to escape from a tight squeeze. First attach 2-inch-thick (5 cm) wooden blocks to the wall for support, then attach the trellis to the blocks.

Grid lock

Few gardeners will admit to erecting chain-link fences, yet they are everywhere, neatly

Fine vines for every occasion

Upper stories

City walls can be intimidating, particularly when they are two-story expanses of brick or stucco; but their breadth and severity is the perfect foil for a vine of great character and dimension. This situation offers one of those moments of artistic tension, when a soft-tissue climber with multiple ornamental features meets up against a hard and massive surface in classic romantic fashion. Vines for completely flat walls must have attributes for climbing and fortitude for holding on in wind and weather.

Boston ivy, *Parthenocissus tricuspidata,* zone 4, sun to bright shade
Virginia creeper, *P. quinquefolia,* zone 4, sun to bright shade
Silver-vein creeper, *Parthenocissus henryana,* zone 8, light shade
English ivy, *Hedera helix,* zone 5, sun to shade
Climbing hydrangea, *Hydrangea petiolaris,* zone 4, sun to shade

Smaller perennial vines for arbors, trellises and walls

Clematis hybrids and species, zone 4, sun to light shade, also can be grown in trees and shrubs
Kolomikta vine, *Actinidia kolomikta,* zone 4, sun to part shade, foliage is variegated with pink and white
Honeysuckle hybrids and species, zone 4, sun to part shade, scented flowers
Trumpet creeper, *Campsis radicans,* zone 4, sun, self-clinging to walls

Late-blooming clematis

'Gypsy Queen', 'Hagley Hybrid', 'Jackmanii', 'Lady Betty Balfour', 'Pink Fantasy', 'Rouge Cardinal', 'Star of India', 'Ville de Lyon', sweet autumn clematis (*C. terniflora*), 'Bill Mackenzie', 'Radar Love' (*C. tangutica*), 'Etoile Violette', 'Little Nell', 'Polish Spirit', 'Duchess of Albany', 'Gravetye Beauty'.

Summer annual vines

Unlike winter-hardy vines, these summer-flowering vines live for just one season and climb fences, trellises and arbors. Most are sensitive to frost and are treated as annuals in northern regions, where they can be grown in planting beds or containers. Some vines are perennial in the south, where they may die to the ground in winter, resprouting in spring.

Blue passion-flower, *Passiflora caerulea,* 10 to 20 feet (3 to 6 m), sun, perennial in zone 8
Chilean jasmine, *Mandevilla suaveolens,* 10 to 20 feet (3 to 6 m), sun, pink (*M.* x *amoena* 'Alice du Pont') or white, perennial in zone 10
Canary creeper, *Tropaeolum peregrinum,* 6 to 8 feet (1.8 to 2.4 m), light shade, yellow, annual vine preferring moist soil
Cup-and-saucer vine, *Cobaea scandens,* 10 to 20 feet (3 to 6 m), sunny location in cool regions, part shade in warm regions, violet and white, perennial in zone 9
Moonflower, *Ipomoea alba,* 6 to 8 feet (1.8 to 2.4 m), sun and warmth, night-blooming white and fragrant
Sweet pea, *Lathyrus odoratus,* 4 to 6 feet (1.2 to 1.8 m), sun and cool location, many colors and some highly scented, annual vine
Confederate jasmine (star jasmine), *Trachelospermum jasminoides,* 8 to 10 feet (2.4 to 3 m), light shade and moist soil, scented white flowers in spring and sporadically through summer, perennial in zone 9

locking gardeners inside their private territories. This fencing offers little in the way of beauty or privacy, and invites the accumulation of drifting garbage and wet laundry. However, as a structure for plant growth, its possibilities are many.

For privacy, the familiar Dutchman's pipe, also known as pipe vine (*Aristolochia durior*, zone 4, sun to part shade), is fondly recalled as an effective screen on many old-fashioned verandas. Its heart-shaped or kidney-shaped leaves overlap in neatly arranged shingle fashion, and given a rough wooden form to climb, it will provide complete coverage in the first season. Its woody twining stems will make a dense covering for trellises, arbors, pergolas and dreaded chain-link fences. The unusual yellow-green tubular flowers appear in May to June and are followed by pods containing seeds. Dutchman's pipe can travel 20 to 30 feet (6 to 9 m) in two seasons and will grow well in full sun to part shade. It needs consistently moist soil, and wilts sadly in drought.

Another good choice for privacy is silver lace vine, also called fleece-vine (*Polygonum aubertii*, zone 4, sun to part shade), particularly where screening is desired on a chain-link fence or a board fence with a trellis panel at the top. Silver lace is a vigorous and gleeful plant that seems forever laughing, and is most attractive when allowed to grow unrestrained, as much of its beauty is in the aggressive twining movement of the many slender stems. It rolls along impetuously and can achieve 10 to 15 feet (3 to 4.5 m) in one growing season, cre-ating quite a commotion of delicate apple-green leaves and cascades of charmingly fragrant, lacy white flowers in late summer, when they are much appreciated. Its ebullient nature is useful in small gardens where there is an expanse of fence-line territory to cover. If allowed to travel unrestrained, it can reach 25 to 35 feet (7.5 to 10.5 m) over several seasons. Silver lace vine grows well in almost any location and is tolerant of dry soils. When too closely confined, it may leap onto neighboring plants, but its tendrils are easily removed.

Also a good candidate for chain-link fences or on a trellis is fiveleaf akebia (*Akebia quinata*, zone 4, sun to part shade), an ornamental vine with intriguing bluish green foliage and dangling clusters of bicolored fragrant blossoms, chocolate purple and rosy purple, in spring. The five-lobed leaves have a delicate appearance and are evergreen in warm climates and deciduous in the north. Akebia adapts to wet or dry soil, in either sun or shade. It is capable of traveling 20 to 40 feet (6 to 12 m), but will be less aggressive in shade, and is also more restrained in northern climates. It is a good ground cover as well and will mask an unsightly object or area, although in southern regions the vine has enough vigor to gobble up large tracts of real estate. Its slender woody stems are easily confined when it's grown on a trellis or arbor, and it can be cut to the ground in late winter for complete control if necessary.

Two good scrambling vines for chain-link fences, trellis or ground cover are perennial sweet pea (*Lathyrus latifolius*, zone 5, sun)

*Chain-link fences are common markers of city lot lines, and gardeners must make the best of them. Vines of all kinds and climbing roses can be splendidly displayed along fence surfaces. Bending the rose canes horizontally and tying them in place will activate many more flowering buds than if they are allowed to grow vertically. This old garden rose blooms behind the prominent flowers of biennial clary sage (*Salvia sclarea, *zone 5*), curly stems of garlic and the straight stand of peas.*

and Japanese honeysuckle (*Lonicera japonica* 'Halliana', zone 5, sun to shade), both long blooming and tolerant of dry soil. The usual climate influences apply: both are smaller and restrained in the north, rambunctious and galloping in the south. These are cottage garden plants with good draping qualities, and they look well when masking angular corners or softening a rough form or fence.

Food of the gods

Grape vines are ancient and noble plants, and their fruit was considered a favorite treat with celestial deities of Roman and Greek mythology. Grown for ornamental purposes, they require only a long run to display their elegant naturalism in all seasons. A stretch of simple post-and-wire fencing down the long side of a garden is a good place to let a grape vine stretch out. A shady pergola over a patio or deck is also a traditional structure for the cascading leaves and fruit.

Any grape vine is worth having and will provide food for birds and, after annual pruning in late winter, lengths of cane for wreath making. Vines with particular ornamental features include *Vitis* 'Brant' (zone 5), a plant with strong cold-hardiness and chartreuse leaves held tightly together in early spring, then opening to medium green with a pattern of red and copper; and crimson glory vine (*V. coignetiae*, zone 5), with unusual rounded foliage and bright crimson color in autumn. In southern zones, any of the Muscadine grapes can adorn a fence with leaves that turn bright golden at season's end.

Reluctant bloomer

Wisteria is a vine that knows how to sulk. At maturity its massive weight and form require heavy-duty support on an overhead pergola or strong fence, where it may languish in a beautiful display of foliage but produce no blooms. A bit of tough love with the pruning shears is the most successful method to trigger flower buds: in late winter before spring growth begins, cut each off-shoot from the main vine back to two to four buds. When buds begin to swell in spring, feed the vine with one application of water-soluble 10-52-10 fertilizer that contains a big dose of phosphorus to encourage flower buds.

Heady scents

Japanese wisterias (*Wisteria floribunda*, zone 5) are such beautiful vines that it seems unnecessary to gild the lily. But although most wisteria blossoms have some degree of scent, certain plants possess more than their share of intoxicating spring fragrance. The most notable selections include 'Ivory Tower' (white), 'Longissima Alba' (white), 'Macrobotrys' (reddish violet to violet) and 'Rosea' (pale rose, tipped purple).

Wisteria is a massive woody vine that can lift the roof from a house, and requires very strong support for its clinging trunk and branches. This vine is pruned so that all its leaf surface is on top of the pergola, increasing exposure to sunlight. Maximum length of flower racemes is achieved by fertilizing with compost, aged manure or a low-nitrogen plant food in late autumn after leaves have dropped.
Too much nitrogen causes wisteria to make leafy growth and forget about flowering. Prune young tendrils and branches in late winter, cutting back to two or three buds. Immediately after spring flowering is finished (or in June if the vine hasn't flowered), fertilize with superphosphate to encourage flower bud set for next year.

Five

Lawns and ground covers

Covering the earth

Nature abhors bare soil. Left to the capable cycles of the natural world, bare soil is converted to a young meadow within the span of one growing season. Anyone who has turned the earth of a flower bed in early spring and returned ten days later to find it carpeted with a stand of weed seedlings well understands the efficiency of this system. Left undisturbed, those tender seedlings will assume a permanent status in the order of plant hierarchy. Their emergence is a sure signal that, given the tiniest crack of light, wild plants will eventually prevail over the well-laid surfaces of urban builders. Extraordinary amounts of time and money are devoted to technologies, chemicals and materials to inhibit the growth of indigenous plants, but still the wild grasses grow, and always will.

The need to cover the earth is common to both city and country gardeners. For both, the plant of choice for open spaces has traditionally been the grass lawn. Serviceable and resilient, able to withstand foot traffic and cushion falls, the lawn of hybrid grass plants is a good suppressor of indigenous weed seeds lying buried in the soil. The system of suppression works well as long as the lawn is kept healthy and strong with frequent attention; but left to their own devices, hybrids such as Kentucky bluegrass are weak competitors against their more aggressive ancestors waiting just below soil level.

Establishing lawn areas around a residence has a long history. Twelfth-century scythed lawns were used as perimeter zones outside castle moats to alert homeowners of surprise visitors. Contemporary lawns are most often buffers between the public road and neighboring properties, and a psychological device to create a comfort zone of uniformity. Lawns also have design purposes, connecting areas and organizing space. And of course, mown grasses are great recreational surfaces for sports, children's play equipment and social activities. Having a lawn, or usually two, is taken for granted in most single-family dwellings, where outdoor activity requires something soft to walk on.

Lawns also are closely associated with a nostalgic reassurance that one element in life is consistent. The vision of wind rippling through the "long tall grass of home" is a classic North American emblem of ancestry. The images of summer dew and autumn frost lying on the grass are important seasonal associations, and the fragrance of new-mown grass combined with the comforting whir of the push-mower is a deeply etched sensory memory. Although power mowers and leaf blowing machines are more in keeping with contemporary reality, these associations still feed our perception of grass.

A closer look at front lawns on residential streets quickly reveals the diversity of quality and success with which lawns are grown. Despite the broad acceptance of turf grasses as useful plants for covering soil, there apparently is considerable difficulty in maintaining common standards. And there are reasons why.

Previous page: The lawn of your dreams might be a velvet golf-green, but keeping it that way is going to require lots of time, equipment and chemicals. Settling for a less than ideal lawn, but definitely better than a rough playing field, still satisfies the desire for an expanse of luxuriant grass. Fertilizing twice a year and leaving the clippings in place go a long way toward elevating the quality of a simple lawn, with time to spare in the chair watching it grow.

Dawn of a new lawn

Lawns of the late twentieth century are based on a golf-course aesthetic of velvet consistency, lush texture and admittance to members only. They are limited combinations of selected hybrids, genetically remote from their coarse-tissue ancestors, and have traded off most of their traits of self-preservation for a glamorous appearance. On the prairie, they would never make it to the end of the season.

Modern hybrid grasses are soft and succulent, and those qualities alone seriously affect their ability to function well in the presence of insects, disease pathogens and environmental stress. They do not make strong root growth in the low-fertility, compacted soils found in most city gardens, and they are frequently overwhelmed by wild grasses and weeds. Hybrid grasses require a high-nitrogen diet to boost their vigor, and quickly go dormant in mid-summer drought. They make their best appearance when their height is kept under 2 inches (5 cm), and this low mowing proportionately decreases root length and increases the evaporation of the soil moisture on which they are dependent.

Hot and cold grasses

Turf grasses can be divided into warm- and cool-season species. The familiar mix of Kentucky bluegrass, ryegrass and fescue produces cool-season plants, which prefer a growing season within the range of 40°F to 85°F (5°C to 30°C), although it will become dormant and recover well after extreme heat.

In southern regions, where heat and humidity extremes are frequent and prolonged, warm-season grasses are better choices for green lawns that won't sizzle up in summer weather. Bermuda grass, centipede grass, St. Augustine grass and zoysia grass are all high-performance growers in big heat and humidity. Centipede grass grows well in part shade, as do some of the hybrids of St. Augustine grass and zoysia grass. All are drought-hardy, and zoysia grass tolerates exceptionally heavy traffic. These grass species are resilient in both dry heat and humid, tropical conditions within the range of 55°F to 110°F (13°C to 43°C); they become brown and dormant when the temperature falls below 55°F (13°C).

Lawn seed mixes

Most turf grass seed mixes contain three seeds. Kentucky bluegrass is a cool-season grass that tends to turn brown and go dormant in mid-summer heat. It recuperates quickly from injury, but competes poorly with weeds. Plenty of water and fertilizer are necessary to maintain its blue-green color. But the extra moisture and nitrogen invite fungus infections and the accumulation of an excessively thick layer of organic debris, called thatch, which prevents oxygen from reaching the root zone.

The shortcomings of Kentucky bluegrass are somewhat compensated for by the presence of such tougher species as ryegrass. Turf-type perennial ryegrasses produce a medium-textured stand of grass that is quick to establish and adapts well to periods of drought. Unlike Kentucky bluegrass, which has a slow start from seed (up to twenty-one days to germination) and cannot compete with weeds in the seedling stage, ryegrass is robust and vigorous immediately after germination. It germinates rapidly, in five to seven days at low temperatures, and consequently is a strong choice for establishing or mending a lawn quickly. It wears well in areas of high foot traffic, is effective in preventing soil erosion on slopes, requires less nitrogen and irrigation than most other turf grasses and performs reasonably well in light shade.

Water-saving grasses

With the many reasons for conserving moisture, a seed mix containing 50 percent perennial ryegrass, 40 percent Kentucky bluegrass and 10 percent white clover should be successfully drought-hardy. Kentucky bluegrass doesn't compete well with other grasses, but it is not required to dominate in this water-saving lawn. The lower proportion of bluegrass contributes just enough deep color and turf-healing ability. For a lawn in shade, substituting Chewings fescue for the Kentucky bluegrass would be appropriate. The seeds will need consistent soil moisture to get started, but will develop into a drought-hardy lawn.

Because of its low nitrogen requirement, ryegrass does not accumulate a problematic thatch layer.

The third grass likely to be found in combination seed mixes is fine-leafed fescue, capable of establishing a deep green turf in conditions of dry shade but equally able to grow well in sun. Fescue is very drought-tolerant and ideal for cottage and vacation properties, but it will not perform well in water-logged, poorly drained soils. It is the turf grass of choice for sandy, poor-fertility soils and for lawns with heavy foot traffic and low management levels. It is likely to decline when subjected to high irrigation and fertilizers too high in nitrogen.

Gardening with grass

GRASSES AND pH
Some species of grass adapt to extremes of soil pH. Bent grass, fescue and the native poverty grass (also know as June grass or white oat grass, *Danthonia spicata*) tolerate acid soils with low pH. Kentucky bluegrass is also somewhat tolerant of low pH. Bermuda grass tolerates both alkaline soil with high pH and salt.

SEEDING A LAWN
New lawns can be seeded from April until late May and from late August through early October. The autumn is preferable because ground moisture is more certain to be available and fewer weeds will be germinating. In the south,

lawns are seeded only in autumn to allow young plants a long cool season before the big heat hits.

Lightly dig over the seed bed, remove stones and debris and incorporate peat moss and manure into the top 6 inches. Use a stiff rake to level the surface and break up any clods of earth into a fine texture. Sow the seed thickly at the rate of 1 lb. (500 g) to every 150 sq. ft. (15 m²). If a roller is available, pass it over the seed to ensure good contact with the soil. Spread compost or a combination of peat moss and manure uniformly over the seed just to cover and then wet the area down with a fine spray. Repeat the spray each day until the seedlings are well established. Don't mow the new grass plants until they are a third taller than desired.

QUICK STARTS

Seeds for different kinds of grass plants germinate at various rates. Bluegrass cultivars are slow to start, and may take eighteen to twenty-one days before seedlings emerge. Ryegrass and fescue are quick to germinate and will be up and green in five to seven days.

Turf grasses are perennial plants and always germinate well after a cold period. Putting the bag of seed in the freezer overnight and planting the next day gives the seeds a bit of artificial winter and enhances speedy germination.

The clover debate

Most lawns more than thirty years old contain a proportion of clover. There was a time when low-growing white clover (*Trifolium repens*) was automatically added to turf grass seed mixes for its ability to fix nitrogen and to remain green when turf grasses are inclined to go brown and dormant. The development of pesticides necessary to treat the weaknesses of succulent bluegrass hybrids damaged the clover and it was removed from seed mixes, diminishing the strength of more contemporary lawns, which contain only turf grasses.

White clover helps lawns by grabbing nitrogen from the air and fixing it as a solid in the soil, where it nourishes not only itself but also the grass plants growing nearby. A low-maintenance lawn containing white clover is capable of feeding itself and will never need supplemental fertilizers to maintain a deep green color. The ability of clover to withstand drought is legendary; it will remain green within a brown and dormant lawn in extended mid-summer heat.

Turf grass purists are quick to point out that clover disrupts the consistent and uniform appearance of a lawn, and this is true if the area is examined on hands and knees. However, from more elevated vantage points, little difference in appearance and texture is visible. If left uncut to a height of 4 inches (10 cm) or more, clover will produce the charac-

This healthy lawn is clearly feeling serious encroachment from robust beds of roses and perennials. Turf grasses and roses share similar appetites for adequate oxygen in the root zone, organic foods like compost and manure, and a consistent supply of moisture. When these needs are met, plants are able to excel without big doses of manufactured fertilizers and chemical pesticides.

teristic white flowers so attractive to honey-bees, but when it's grown in a mix of lawn grasses the standard mowing height will ensure the flower buds are consistently removed.

Clover camouflage

City lawns often have patches of bare soil caused by chronically dry and compacted conditions. Lawn grasses recede from these areas, leaving them vacant and exposed to the elements. White clover is quick to colonize these spaces and can successfully resurrect a city lawn laid low by urban conditions.

In early spring when nights are still frosty, combine 2 parts peat moss and 1 part sharp builder's sand as a carrier for the seed, and mix in white clover seed, allowing ½ lb. to 1 lb. (250 g to 500 g) per 1,000 sq. ft. (100 m²). Thoroughly rake or scratch up the soil in bare patches and hand-broadcast the mix of seeds, peat moss and sand across the entire lawn, being sure to cover the vacant areas. If spring conditions are wet, rain will provide sufficient moisture; if the soil is dry, water the seeds in with a light spray.

City pests

Gardeners are never alone. Swarms of wildlife pass through a city garden, usually unnoticed. It is impossible to keep them out, and gardeners need to learn tolerance when plant damage is apparent. The industry and antics of a leaf-cutter bee are so extraordinary it is worth giving over a portion of tender foliage to the event. While many insects and animals are a joy to behold, though, some others can become a nuisance. But using excessively toxic chemicals to address pest problems is a risk not worth taking. Pesticides kill all living things.

Squirrels are more entertaining than television, but you won't find them amusing when they eat your crocus and tulip bulbs. To keep them from disturbing any kind of garden area, plant crown imperial (*Fritillaria imperialis*) bulbs in autumn. This fist-sized bulb has a strong aroma of skunk, and squirrels can smell it through the soil and will give wide berth to the area. Humans will barely notice the perfume once it's buried, and the impres-

Seeing nitrogen

To see the clover plant at work converting nitrogen from the air into a solid form, wait until mid-summer and find a large, healthy clump. Carefully dig out a mature plant and gently shake the soil from the roots. Dip them in water to remove as much soil as possible. Lay the plant and its root system on a piece of paper and look for tiny beige nodules attached to the roots. These little bumps are the source of nitrogen and are feeding the clover and surrounding grass plants. Clover is able to accomplish this alchemy only with the assistance of *Rhizobium*, a beneficial bacteria that lives on the roots of legume plants. The amount of nitrogen nodules increases when the soil has good structure and sufficient oxygen in the root zone.

sive spring flower is astounding. Allow the foliage to ripen after the flower is finished in spring and next year it will return. Squirrels can smell it any time the ground isn't frozen. The bulbs are expensive, but only one is needed for a small garden bed approximately twenty feet long.

Raccoons are amiable creatures who know they were here first, but they're willing to share. They are attracted to any kind of food left in the open, and have engineering skills for opening even locked garbage cans. It may be necessary to house cans in a shed or garage to keep them secure. Raccoons have little interest in perennial plants, but will lift the lawn overnight in search of white grubs, the larvae of various beetles. Despite the horrific damage they cause in a grub-frenzy, the lawn is easily repaired.

Perennial plants, shrubs and trees maintain normal and necessary associations with insects and diseases, and only a few are life threatening. If particular ornamental plants or vegetables are repeatedly afflicted by pests, it is better to eliminate these plants from the garden than to begin a spray program. Some insects, such as green aphids, are easily brushed off stems. If you don't want to touch them, wear rubber gloves or aim a stream of water at them. The aphids don't have enough sense to find their way back.

Ants are community-spirited insects and they can make large colonies in lawns that are excessively dry. They can't swim and will go far to avoid water, so keeping the lawn wet will usually discourage their mounds. Ants love to inhabit the air spaces made in the roots of shrubs that are never irrigated. This visitation is a special punishment for gardeners who have been negligent in supplying water to a hedge. Sprinkle large ant hills with Borax or pour hot peppermint tea over them. Both are toxic to ants.

If pest problems go beyond your level of tolerance and some method of intervention is necessary, always choose the least toxic chemical that will do the job. Organic pesticides are effective and have short residual lives after spraying, making them less dangerous in the environment. If black spot on roses and mildew on phlox are anticipated, spray them each week with a solution of 1 heaping teaspoon (5 mL) of baking soda (sodium bicarbonate) in 2 quarts (2L) of water. A weekly spray with liquid sulfur is also effective. Spot diseases on Japanese maples and fungus on grapes can be treated with Bordo Mix, which contains fixed copper compounds.

Investigating lawn bugs

Most often turf-chewing insects are safely in hiding before the effects of their damage are evident, but there are clues the gardener can use to figure out who the culprits might be. Irregular patches of dead, straw-colored grass appearing in mid-summer could be the work of chinchbugs, but similar damage is also caused by the larvae of three kinds of beetles,

European chafer, Japanese beetle and May/ June beetle.

Grasp some of the dead grass strands and gently pull them. If they come easily up and appear to be disconnected from the roots, the insect is likely one of the beetle larvae that feed on turf grass roots in spring and again in autumn. The chemicals to deal with this kind of soil insect are very toxic and remain on the lawn for several weeks after application. It is preferable to rent a core aeration machine to pull out small plugs of turf in spring or autumn, upsetting larvae and eggs. Afterwards apply beneficial nematodes, available from garden centers. The nematodes are microscopic worms that will feed on any larvae that remain.

However, if you feel resistance when pulling at the dead strands of grass, their roots are probably intact and the damage may have been caused by chinchbugs. Their damage is usually noticed in mid-summer as blotchy dead patches in the lawn. The bugs' presence can be verified by spreading a white handkerchief on green grass adjoining a dead patch and flooding a small area next to it with water. The chinchbugs will attempt to jump on the handkerchief to escape the deluge. Chinchbugs don't like water and most often infest lawns that are chronically dry. Again, it's best to avoid the chemical solution. Keeping the lawn better irrigated will put an end to their interest, and damaged areas can be repaired with seed or sod in early autumn.

A new method of fighting insect infestation in turf grass without resorting to pesticides is to include endophytic grasses in the seed composition of the lawn. Endophytes are a systemic fungus introduced into certain species of grass and living in tissues of the leaf and stem. Grass seed infected with endophytes is resistant to invasion of some turf grass pests, including sod webworm, bluegrass billbug and black beetle. Infected grasses also show increased resistance to mid-summer heat and drought, quicker green recovery after dormancy, and reduced weed invasion. Seeds of endophytic perennial ryegrasses, tall fescue and fine-leafed fescues can be purchased from garden centers and seed companies and sprinkled over a lawn in autumn. The endophytic grasses are safe for people and domestic pets but are somewhat injurious to grazing pasture animals.

About pesticides

Horticultural chemicals will definitely fulfill their promise to eliminate an undesirable

Slug boundaries

Slugs are most active from 10 PM to 4 AM, just when gardeners are least likely to be on patrol. To keep slugs off plants at any time, sprinkle a generous circle of powdered sulfur on the soil around plants that are showing slug damage. The sulfur burns the slugs and they won't cross the band of powder. Sulfur is harmless to the soil, other curious animals and your bare skin. It should be renewed after a heavy rainfall.

insect, plant or disease organism. They are, however, also dangerous to the people who apply them. Many synthetic pesticides were developed as agents of chemical warfare during World War II with the intent to kill people. Despite their easy availability, it is a mistake to assume they are safe to use.

Pesticides are dangerous not only when they are handled and mixed. Most synthetic chemicals have a residual life that continues long after the day of application. Common synthetic insecticides such as carbaryl, malathion and diazinon may remain in the soil for up to twelve weeks. Herbicides applied as sprays or combined with fertilizers can also linger for long periods. Weed killers like dicamba may persist for two to twelve months, 2,4-D and 2,4,5-T for one to five months. Arsenic leached from green pressure-treated wood remains in the soil indefinitely. And all chemicals applied to lawns will find their way into the water table.

Of the many creatures and organisms roaming the garden, only 10 percent of them are inclined to damage ornamental plants. The other 90 percent are necessary parts of the ecological life of every garden. But blanket coverage of the lawn with pesticides will kill everything and set the stage for a major environmental hazard.

In the nineteenth century, overuse of arsenic and nicotine sulfate, a home-brewed insecticide, killed many gardeners. Twentieth-century synthetic pesticides are the cause of cancers, central nervous system disorders,

kidney and liver failure and sterility. Each time you spray the lawn, you absorb an amount of the pesticide through skin, nose and mouth. If you walk over a lawn that has been sprayed with pesticide, some amount of the chemical will be carried into the house on your shoes. Some pesticides have a cumulative effect, collecting in body fat and eventually amounting to a dangerous dose.

Organic insecticides act quickly when they're sprayed directly on insects but lose their toxicity within a day, making them preferable to lingering synthetic chemicals. Pyrethrum and rotenone will control almost any insect on ornamental plants, and can be used on vegetables up to the day of harvest. Both are organic poisons made from plants. Use these insecticides only when absolutely necessary, for they will kill the good bugs, too.

Weeds are opportunistic plants and will eventually overwhelm a weak lawn. The best way to keep weeds out of lawns is to strengthen the grass with organic fertilizer and good care. Weeds are not vermin. It isn't a scandal to have some in the lawn, and you can develop your own strategy to control them. Try turning a blind eye to the small weeds and digging out only the large ones. This will effectively keep them from developing into colonies.

PRE-EMERGENT DANGERS

Pre-emergent herbicides are chemicals designed to prevent seeds from germinating. They are used most often to prevent the seeds of crabgrass and other weeds from sprouting in either spring or autumn. These chemicals are powerful germination inhibitors and will prevent any seeds, including hybrid lawn grasses, flowers and vegetables, from germinating. They are effective up to eight weeks after application. If you intend to over-seed a lawn to thicken it in spring or autumn, be sure not to use pre-emergent herbicide to control weeds that season.

Crabgrass is an annual weed grass that produces prolific amounts of seeds in late summer. These remain on the ground until the spring, when they will germinate. Most lawns have a bit of crabgrass, and the best method of control is to dig out large clumps of it and patch the areas with grass seed or sod; keep the lawn mown to 3 inches (7.5 cm), effectively shading the seeds and preventing germination. By keeping the lawn a little drier, you will further discourage crabgrass seeds from germinating.

What makes lawns tick

Taking a deep breath

Since most lawns lie on top of compacted clay soil that is deficient in oxygen, the roots are unable to penetrate deeply and plants lack energy and show poor growth. The best way to inject oxygen into the root zone is by core aeration every second year in spring or autumn, and annually if your soil is severely compacted. Coring machines can be rented by hands-on gardeners, and some lawn service companies perform this service. The coring machine is pushed along like a mower, cutting thousands of thin holes through the turf and into the soil below. After coring, mix 1 inch (2.5 cm) of sharp builder's sand and 1 inch (2.5 cm) of peat moss together (use the formula on page 53). Spread the mixture over the lawn and sweep it across the turf with a soft leaf rake. As this mixture falls into the holes, it will begin to change the character of the soil under the lawn, breaking up compaction and bringing organic material and oxygen into the root zone.

As for the cores of soil that the machine tosses on the ground, sweep them along with the rake, breaking them up slowly, and then leave them to compost in place and sink back down into the lawn as an organic mulch. Core aeration and amending with organic materials is a bit messy for about ten days but well worth the temporary aesthetic upheaval. It can be done at any time the ground is not frozen, but the aesthetic disruption is least noticed in autumn. Core aeration enhances the growth and health of a lawn far better than fertilizer.

Lawns over sandy soils have the opposite problem: too much air in a dry, infertile soil deficient in organic material. This turf benefits from being mulched three times a season with finely shredded organic amendments like leaves, compost, aged manure and peat moss. Rake these materials through the lawn to a depth of no more than 1 inch (2.5 cm). Watering will settle the materials and encourage the grass to stand up and assume its regular height. Lawns mulched in this way benefit from the water-holding capability of organic material and also will be insulated from heat and evaporation of moisture. If compost and manure are used, the benefit to fertility will be noticeable within four days as the lawn takes on a deeper green hue.

Sod selection

Sod farms grow very basic varieties of turf grasses. For sunny locations their product contains a high proportion of Kentucky bluegrass (approximately 80 percent), and may even consist exclusively of that cultivar. Sod for shade may need to be specially ordered. It will have a proportion of fine fescue plants in the mix. Custom blending can only be done at home, using individually purchased varieties of seed to establish the lawn. The grass plants purchased in sheets of sod are approximately two years old, intensively fertilized and have the benefit of mature appearance and density. A lawn from sod gives instant coverage and effect but requires the same work and considerations as a lawn made from seed; that is, providing a well prepared bed, applying consistent moisture and staying off the surface until roots are established into the soil.

Pine needle mulch

Pine needles have a rigid form that will not lie perfectly flat or be crushed. They always maintain bits of space that are filled with air. Incorporating them into soil or using them in a mulch is an effective method of introducing oxygen into compacted soil. When installing a new lawn using either sod or seed, include pine needles in the initial soil preparation. Established lawns can be lightly mulched with pine needles in autumn. Sprinkle the needles across the lawn and distribute them evenly with a leaf rake, and they will slide down between the blades to eventually settle at soil level.

Pine needles are excellent organic material and of great value in building good soil structure. While they are acidic when freshly shed from their trees, they are very slow to decompose and will have no appreciable effect on soil pH.

Patching a damaged lawn

Lawns can become patchy with sections of thin grass and bare earth. Many circumstances contribute to this problem: dogs, frequent foot traffic, tree roots, low light, inadequate moisture, compacted soil, insect damage, fertilizer burn or low fertility.

- To repair bare spots in the lawn using grass seed, rake away all dead roots and strands of grass, and rake a second time to scratch up the soil and create a soft bed for the seed. Select a grass suited to the light conditions in the garden, and sprinkle it generously over the bare spot. Cover the seed with a 1-inch (2.5 cm) layer of damp peat moss to envelope it in a moisture-retentive mulch. Water the patched area with a gentle spray, and keep it wet until after the seeds have germinated. Cut the new grass when it is 3 inches (7.5 cm) high. Do not fertilize for six weeks. Grass seeds germinate best in the cool weather of autumn (up to four weeks before hard frost) and spring.

- To repair bare spots in the lawn using sod, use a blunt-nosed spade to cut a square or rectangle in the turf. Hold the spade horizontally and push it forcefully under the patch of turf to cut the roots. Lift off the severed section of grass and rake the area to remove any debris and make a soft bed for the new sod. Use a sharp knife to cut the sod strip to fit the area and set it in, butting the edges closely and trimming away any overlaps. The seams should be close but still allow space for your fingertips to slightly poke in. Use a roller to settle the sod and drive out air pockets, or lay a board over the area and stand on it. Water the sod each day for two weeks, and cut the new grass when it is 3 (7.5 cm) inches high. Do not fertilize for four weeks.

- To thicken a thin lawn, core aerate the area with a rented machine. Break up the plugs of grass with a leaf rake and spread them across the lawn. Broadcast grass seed, choosing a variety suited to the available light, and cover it with a 1-inch (2.5 cm) mulch of equal parts peat moss and aged manure. Keep the lawn wet with a daily watering until the new grass plants are well established.

Laying a sod lawn

Sod needs to rest on a carefully prepared bed to get good root growth into the soil. If the soil is compacted, dig it over thoroughly and incorporate sharp builder's sand to break up the clay. Two to four bales of 6-cubic-foot-size peat moss per 100 square feet should also be incorporated into the soil to make a soft and moist bed for the grass. Compost, manure or an organic granular fertilizer with low analysis (such as 5-10-5) can be added for nutrition.

Rake and grade the area to a fine texture, breaking up clods and mixing in amendments. The area should be completely prepared before the sod arrives, and you can even finish the day before the lawn is to be laid. Stack the sod in the shade, out of direct sunlight, and protect it from wind with a tarp or burlap if necessary.

Use the straight line of a bordering pavement or driveway, or run a taught string up the center of the lawn area, and work along this line to establish the first row. Use a rake to smooth out footsteps in the soil just before each strip of sod is laid down. Joints should be tightly butted without overlapping. Use a sharp knife to cut the sod strips where they meet an edge or need to be fitted into irregular angles. If working on a slope, wooden pegs may be necessary to hold the sod in place until roots are extended into the soil.

Run a lightweight roller over the finished lawn to make sure the grass roots are in contact with soil, and water daily for the first week, three times in the second week and once weekly thereafter. The newly sodded lawn will need mowing after about a week.

Mowing

Each blade of grass is an important site for the process of photosynthesis and the manufacture of plant carbohydrate foods. By cutting the blades short, you truncate these production areas, leaving less tissue to carry on food production and affecting every function of the plants. Keeping the lawn consistently short (below 2 inches (5 cm) in blade length) introduces serious hazards for the collective health and longevity of the lawn. The roots of grass plants grow in direct proportion to blade length. Blades less than 2 inches (5 cm) high will foster shallowly rooted plants unable to reach groundwater, exposing the roots to high temperatures near the surface of the soil.

Short blades not only inhibit production of energy, they are also unable to shade the soil from scorching sun. As the soil environment becomes hotter and drier in mid-summer, it is often an ideal site for chinchbug activity. As well, excessive light reaching the soil enables the seeds of broadleaf weeds and crabgrass to germinate and compete with the turf grass. The short blade length ultimately weakens the lawn and predisposes it to significant weed and insect invasion, and that in turn leads to consideration of pesticides to deal with these problems. This scenario is one of gardening's great snowballs, picking up ever more problems as it rolls along.

The whole thing can be easily avoided by raising the blade height of the mower. By allowing the grass to stand 2 to 3 inches (5 to 7.5 cm) tall, the root length will be deeper, allowing access to reserves of groundwater; the soil surface will be shaded, lowering temperature in the root zone and preventing the germination of weed seeds, and enough blade tissue will be available to keep up a productive hum of photosynthetic activity.

Keep the mower's blades sharp to avoid the ragged blade tips that result from a dull cutting edge. Ragged cuts are slow to heal, allowing disease pathogens to easily enter the plants

Knowing how much lawn is enough leaves space for planting something different. Power mowers perform best on flat surfaces – even gentle slopes eventually develop a ragged appearance. This boulevard strip could have been planted with grass and forgotten except for weekly mowing. But as an ornamental bed it is a changing seasonal feature giving pleasure to everyone on the road. The display of tulips, daffodils, violas and grape hyacinths lights up this city block for an extended spring show, and is changed to hot-colored plants in early summer.

and infect the lawn. Many hardware stores will sharpen mower blades, and in spring blade-sharpening services operating from vans cruise some neighborhoods.

Mow frequently so that no more than a third of the blade length is removed at one time, ensuring enough tissue is left to carry on making energy for the plants.

Making a mowing strip

A messy edge ruins the appearance of a well-cut lawn. Hand-cutting the edge with shears is tedious and time consuming, and although the nylon-filament string-trimmers are quick to do the job, they add to the noise pollution of a serene garden. Installing a mowing strip of bricks between the edge of the lawn and a flower bed ensures the mower blades will cut the edge.

Sink a row of paving bricks side by side into the edge of the lawn so that their tops are level with the soil. The mower wheel will go right over the bricks and the blade will cleanly cut the edge of the grass. The mowing strip saves time and work and helps to organize space in the garden.

Irrigation

Everything grows better with sufficient moisture, delivered by a regularly scheduled long drink of water. Turf grass requires 1 inch (2.5 cm) of water a week to maintain a strong stand of grass. During cool weather that amount of moisture may readily be available in the soil, and watering isn't necessary. As temperatures rise and more moisture evaporates from the soil surface, water reserves in the soil may be insufficient, and irrigation becomes necessary.

The most important consideration in delivering irrigation is that enough water penetrates deeply. Slowing the rate at which water is delivered makes a substantial contribution to deep penetration. Setting the sprinkler lower will cover less lawn but allows water to slowly penetrate a compacted soil and prevents runoff.

It's best to water once a week, slowly over

Let them lie

Grass clippings allowed to fall back into the lawn and compost in place become a valuable mulch for the soil, and they have nutritional value, too. The clippings from a healthy lawn will meet a third of the lawn's nutritional requirements for each growing season. The fertilizer values of fresh green grass clippings are 0.5 percent nitrogen, 0.2 percent phosphorus and 0.5 percent potassium, and that is comparable to the analysis of worm castings.

If quantities of fresh green grass clippings are available, use them to amend soil deficient in organic material and fertility. For every 1,000 square feet (305 sq. m) of soil, spread 300 lb. (136 kg) of green clippings and dig them in. For full nutritional value, the clippings must be fresh and green, but they are still a good source of organic fiber if they're dried out. If you're amending the soil of a food garden, don't use clippings from a lawn that has been sprayed with herbicides.

many hours, so that the water can penetrate to below root level and keep root systems growing downward. Rather than watering a lawn five times a week for forty-five minutes each time, it's better to supply one long, slow watering for three hours and forty-five minutes. Short periods of irrigation several times a week will only moisten the surface soil and keep roots shallow and therefore vulnerable to heat and drought.

After watering, the soil under the lawn should ideally feel moist at 6 inches (15 cm) and damp at 10 inches (23 cm). Lifting a corner flap of sod, digging a small hole and feeling the soil is a muddy and accurate method of judging how effectively irrigation has penetrated.

A lawn should be irrigated in the morning or early evening, when wind and direct sunlight are less likely to evaporate water. The amount delivered can be monitored by measuring the depth collected in a shallow baking pan placed on the lawn. During a serious drought when emergency restrictions may prohibit irrigation, allowing lawns to go brown and dormant is the best way to ensure a strong green recovery in late summer. Hybrid lawn grasses are moisture-intensive plants requiring excessive amounts of water to remain green during drought conditions. Their best defense against drought is to stop growing and assume a semi-dormant state of brownness until eventual rains bring them back into growth. Seeding drought-hardy white clover (*Trifolium repens*) into your lawn will give it a green appearance through dry

periods. The clover remains green even when the grass browns out.

Nutrients

When plants, like all living things, are fed large amounts of one nutrient or chemical element, they begin to exhibit strange behavior. Grass plants on too much nitrogen are like people on speed: there is an acceleration of life processes and a big crash at the end. Despite

---

Nothing dirty about mushrooms

Lawns growing on water-logged, compacted soils may sprout occasional crops of mushrooms. This phenomenon can also be triggered by extended rainy seasons. Mushrooms are the fruiting bodies of fungus organisms below soil level. Most often the fungus is active on decomposing wood buried beneath the lawn. An older lawn may have tree roots beneath the soil, and a lawn in a new building site probably has construction debris buried underground. Fungus is most active when soil is very wet and drainage is inadequate. The mushrooms are harmless and will disappear when conditions turn drier, and they do make a point of interest as an unusual form of floriferous growth. Mushrooms are not dirty, and they are not weeds.

If mushrooms appear in the lawn where they are not desired, simply go out and kick them over, or let the mower chop them down and the remains will soon disappear. Applying a chemical fungicide to obliterate them will sometimes stain the lawn and injure the turf grass, creating a less interesting spectacle, and the mushrooms will sprout again from their deeply buried underground source.

Needless to say, harvesting and eating any mushroom obtained from the lawn or forest may be a direct route to the sweet hereafter.

this negative effect, advertisements and the media have long advised feeding large amounts of nitrogen to lawns in early spring. Nitrogen is vital to the strong growth of turf grass, but the amounts necessary and the timing of their application have more to do with plant biology than with the gardener's desire for earliest green-up on the block.

Turf grasses require adequate amounts of the three major plant nutrients: nitrogen for deep green color and strong blade growth, phosphorus for aggressive root systems and potassium for hardiness and disease resistance. In addition, the major nutrients work in concert to perform many complex chemical functions of energy production, distribution of carbohydrates and division and replication of cells. Their interdependence is such a strong guideline that supplying only one of the crucial nutrients alone is seldom effective unless the others are represented in at least trace amounts.

When to fertilize lawns

Northeast US and eastern Canada: early June and late October.

Northwest US and western Canada: late May and early November.

Southeast US: early June and late August.

Southwest US: late May and late October.

Midwest US and on the prairies: late May and early November.

If only one feeding is to be given, the best time in any region is in the autumn months of September, October or November.

Providing a conservative amount of supplemental nutrients to give a small enrichment or nudge to the lawn's natural pattern of growth will do no harm to the plants, but administering a major chemical jolt will certainly bring the lawn to grief. In particular, large amounts of nitrogen encourage soft succulent growth favored by insects and fungus diseases. Too much nitrogen also lowers drought tolerance, stressing grass plants by interrupting normal growth patterns, and ultimately weakening the lawn.

MAKING STRONG LAWNS

The smartest feeding strategy is to give the lawn what it needs, when it needs it. Allow the grass to green-up naturally in spring and withhold any feeding until early June, when it's ready to grow aggressively. A 1-inch (2.5 cm) thick mulch of equal parts peat moss and aged animal manure spread with a leaf rake and watered in will provide good nutrients and organic matter. Or a fertilizer product can be used. Manufactured lawn fertilizers with a total nitrogen content of less than 15 percent are acceptable, but organic fertilizers provide a fuller nutritional meal.

Fertilizers with an organic base are now widely available in bagged and packaged form at garden centers, and their contents are listed on the container. Nitrogen is always the first of three numbers in the fertilizer formula that tells what percentage is contained in the nutrient mix. Balanced formulas, like 7-7-7 or 10-10-10, are entirely adequate for almost all garden purposes, as are formulas with varying amounts of nutrients, like 10-6-8. But a manufactured fertilizer with a very high concentration of nitrogen, such as 27-7-7 or 35-5-10, is going to push the lawn toward the brink of disaster. If you are confused by the array of fertilizer products and uncertain what benefit will come from their application, it is better not to use any. The lawn knows what to do, when to do it, and will get on with growing.

FREE FOOD

Manufactured fertilizers are expensive and largely unnecessary. Homemade compost is the best plant food, but is not always available. However, most gardeners can get all the high-quality fertilizer they need for absolutely no cost.

The most reliable and consistent source of nitrogen is produced by leguminous plants. Many herbaceous and woody plants are legumes, but the most useful for fertilizer purposes is white clover (*Trifolium repens*). Many clover plants can be grown in a lawn and between the rows of a vegetable patch. They take gaseous nitrogen from the air and fix it in a solid state in the soil. White clover seed can be purchased in garden centers, usually shelved with grass seed, and through seed catalogues.

An active and prolific worm colony will produce a great abundance of castings that are an ideal form of animal manure, and they will deposit this fertilizer directly at the roots of plants. They are able to make a nutritious manure by ingesting organic material in the soil, in particular from any leaves they find. Allowing leaves to remain on the bare soil throughout the year will insure fat and happy worms, and lots of fertilizer. Worms will accept entire leaves, but shredded leaves are easier for them to handle. Run a lawn mower over the leaves and the pieces will settle between the blades of grass. The worms will then come up to eat them.

Grass clippings are especially rich in nitrogen when fresh and green, and can supply a third of the fertilizer necessary for lawn growth each season.

Stormy weather is a rich source of nitrogen. When lightning flashes across the sky, the electrical charge converts large amounts of gaseous nitrogen into solid form that is brought down to soil level by rain. Watch for a greener lawn two to three days after an electrical storm.

Keeping a lawn of one's own

Healthy grass is a competitive and aggressive grower. If conditions are as close to ideal as possible, grass has the resources to crowd out weeds and resist insect and disease infestation.

A strong start to the new season begins at the end of the old. In late October apply a granular organic-based fertilizer (or acceptable manufactured product) containing nitrogen, phosphorus and potassium. Select a product in which nitrogen, the first number, is

lower than the following two numbers. In cold regions this is a semi-dormant feeding. Grass will have stopped growing but is still green. The nutrients applied now are absorbed by the crown and root system of each grass plant and held for release in early spring. As a result the plants will be able to use the nutrients to best advantage and at an appropriate time in their growth cycle.

In early spring when the turf is firm and dry enough to walk on, rake the lawn well to remove winter debris, dead grass and any accumulated thatch. Take some time to dig out large perennial weeds. Anytime during

The boundary between lawn and terrace is softened by a drift of perennials. Plants are the best judge of suitable growing conditions and will self-sow where circumstances are ideal. Those preferring dry soil with a cool root-run leap from the perennial bed to dry cracks between flagstones. Catmint, perennial geranium, golden feverfew, lady's mantle, thyme, spurge, white fumitory and violets all prefer the austerity of crevice planting. Gardening in the cracks is less work and more fun than the perennial bed.

the spring, apply a 1-inch (25 cm) layer of mulch of equal parts peat moss and aged manure, rake it evenly across the turf and water it in.

Early June is the best time to apply fertilizer for the summer months. Although it is not absolutely necessary, this feeding of supplemental nutrients will help to keep the grass plants competitive with germinating weed seeds. Apply an organic-based granular fertilizer, or an acceptable manufactured product. Select a fertilizer formula in which none of the numbers is greater than 15.

Mow grass frequently to a height between 2 ½ and 3 inches (6 and 7.5 cm), never removing more than a third of the blade length and allowing the clippings to remain on the lawn. Provide irrigation during hot, dry weather and whenever no moisture is present at a depth of 6 inches (15 cm) under the lawn.

Core aerate the lawn every other year in September using a rented machine. Do not use a spiking device for this, as it will only increase compaction. Prepare a mulch of equal parts peat moss and manure and mix in a generous amount of grass seed of a type appropriate to the light and soil conditions of the lawn area. Use a leaf rake to spread it 1-inch (2.5 cm) thick across the turf, and water it in. The over-seeding will thicken the lawn with new plants and help to keep out weeds. Sprinkle the lawn surface each day to ensure the mulch remains moist until new seedling growth is established. Cool and moist nights at this time of year should help to quickly germinate the grass seed.

What to do about thatch

Thatch is an excessively thick layer of organic debris generated by a lawn's rapid growth. When applied too frequently and at too high a concentration, nitrogen fertilizer results in an accumulation of fibrous material and clippings that blocks air from reaching the soil. When the lawn is growing on compacted soil, the thatch problem is intensified. Unlike a normal layer of mulch, this extra-thick, spongy layer is a welcome breeding ground for insects and diseases, and can effectively shut off the flow of moisture and gases into the soil. In an advanced stage, grass plants are forced to root directly into the thatch layer in order to obtain moisture.

Thatch can be raked out with a special rake for this purpose or with a stiff soil rake. If the thatch layer is too thick to be removed with a rake, a verti-cut machine can be used to slice the turf and loosen the layer, and then it can be raked out. The lawn will need to be reseeded and will recover quickly, but withhold nitrogen fertilizers for the duration of the growing season.

Ground cover alternatives

Lawn resentment

Although the ground needs to be covered, there are times and situations when turf grass is not the answer. The growing circumstances may be unsuitable. The space may be too small, or water-saving municipal bylaws may require a drought-hardy alternative. Or a lawn might seem out of place in a stylized downtown courtyard. And there are certain gardeners who gaze on a vivid greensward with unrestrained disappointment, seeing only one kind of plant where many could grow and this is where lawn resentment begins. Gardening is one of the few acceptable venues for an acquisitive spirit, and those who want more plants must have some place to put them. Digging up the lawn is a pragmatic approach to plant collection.

Choosing another method to cover the soil necessarily requires different methods of establishing and managing the plant material. The one feature that distinguishes a lawn from all other ground covers is the extraordinary density of the planting. No other herbaceous or woody plant could survive shoulder-to-shoulder as grass does. The wider spacing of newly installed ground cover leaves viable room for the native plant competitors. The first two to three growing seasons is a bothersome time in the establishment of plants set into bare soil with spaces between them. Serious vigilance is required to keep competitive native grasses and weeds out of the bed, either by hand-digging or by use of a mulch that will not interfere with the spread of the new plants. These things are never as easy as one would hope, but diligence at the beginning pays off with many years of pleasure from a mature planting and, finally, very little maintenance

Density, and plenty of it

What makes a ground cover successful is its density. It doesn't matter how perfectly lovely the foliage and blossom are, if it can't adequately cover the ground it won't protect the soil and suppress the growth of such weeds as plantain and dandelion. To prevent the worst from happening, first, the growth form of the desired plant must be clearly understood, and second, the plants need to be set close enough to have some hope of coming together as a mass in the predictably near future.

Pea gravel is a practical substitute for grass lawn in regions where rainfall is limited and irrigation unavailable. But it also works well as a low-maintenance alternative, eliminating all the tasks associated with lawn care. Gravel comes in various sizes and textures, and a small-size gravel of smooth stones is most pleasant to walk on. Colors also vary, and in this garden the pea gravel is keyed to the color of the roses that bloom all season.

Catalogues will often quote the potential width of a groundcover plant but rarely tell you when that spread might be achieved. Is it three months, or three years? And in what climate, with how many hours of guaranteed direct sunlight?

Cool regions have fewer growing days and less accumulated heat, and plants seldom achieve the same density and coverage as they might in warmer zones. To be successful quickly, a greater number of plants must be installed, and the cost will be proportionately higher. If the catalogue suggests setting the plants 12 inches (30 cm) apart, it would be smart to set them with 8 inches (20 cm) between in a cool garden or one with a lot of shade.

Equally confusing are the light recommendations, so many of which indicate a plant will grow in full sun to part shade. Well, yes, but how fast will it grow? Because sunlight equals energy in plant life, more direct light falling on foliage will result in more energy production and quicker, thicker growth. Less light in partial shade will make proportionately less energy available for covering the earth, and a greater number of plants must be installed to make up the shortfall.

Choosing a ground cover

Sorting groundcover plants into categories — carpets, mats, ramblers, clumps and spreading arches — will help you decide which is suitable.

CARPETS

Where an even covering is required, choose carpeting plants that will roll reliably in all directions and cover whatever is in their way. Among many in this group are the herbaceous sweet woodruff (*Galium odoratum*, zone 5, shade to half sun), with a dazzling white blossom in early spring and charming starry green leaves for ten months of the year; broadleaf evergreen periwinkle (*Vinca minor*, zone 5, sun to half shade), with blue flowers in spring and lustrous foliage year-round, and coniferous 'Blue Rug' juniper (*Juniperus horizontalis* 'Wiltonii', zone 2, sun), a dense and consistent carpet of low blue-green needles.

These plants are all under 10 inches (23 cm) in height, flow smoothly and form a dense carpet over the soil. They are particularly useful surrounding large stones or statuary, and can flow in and around hedges and specimen shrubs. Many forms of carpeting ground covers have the ability to root from their stems as they go along, forming new divisions and colonies.

MATS

Mat-forming plants are also low-growing ground-huggers and behave something like spilled water, spreading out in an irregular shape. Most mats grow from a central crown, although some root from nodes on their stems as they go along, spreading the bounty of their coverage. Familiar to many gardeners are the several forms of bugleweed (*Ajuga reptans*,

zone 3, anywhere except deep shade), which make dense central rosettes that branch out to form colonies of mats in almost any soil. Other families of mats with great charm are the scented ornamental thymes (*Thymus* spp., zone 4, sun) and the spotted dead nettles (*Lamium* spp., zone 4, best in half-day of sun or more), whose miserable name belies their jolly flowers and winsome form. Yet another mat of awesome capability is snow-in-summer (*Cerastium tomentosum*, zone 4, sun), known to most for its small, very gray foliage and lava-like ability to flow over absolutely anything in its path.

*Any low-growing plant with dense coverage can make a lawn, and cold-hardy English ivy (*Hedera helix spp., *zone 5) is a low-maintenance choice for locations with partial sun. Once thickly established, the ivy is beautiful in four seasons and can stand up to occasional foot traffic. Like all ground covers it must be watered and kept weed free until the plants knit together and an organic mulch of shredded leaves or bark can be spread around them to limit weeding time. A small herbal lawn of creeping thyme is an alternative choice for sunny sites, and it tolerates light traffic. But it will want to grow in a mix of equal parts sharp builder's sand, fine gravel and topsoil. Try mat-forming varieties like mother-of-thyme (*Thymus serpyllum, *zone 2), *creeping thyme (*T. praecox, *zone 2) or *T. doerfleri 'Bressingham', *zone 4.*

These mat-forming plants will fill and cover corners in a border and oddly shaped vacant spots in rockeries, and they are especially interesting when allowed to spill out over the edge of a walkway. They don't have quite the meshing power of carpets, which can knit themselves into complete ground covers in larger areas.

RAMBLERS

Rambling groundcover plants have a great urge to travel, most often striking out across the soil, rooting as they go and making new growth off the main line. They will cover lots of territory, but without complete density, and they are most effective when combined with clump-forming plants. A typical rambler is the shrubby cutleaf stephanandra (*Stephanandra incisa* 'Crispa', zone 3, sun to part shade), which forms a fairly dense system of self-rooting woody stems with delicate foliage. One of the taller ground covers, it will grow to about 2 feet (60 cm).

A far more delicately structured plant is creeping jenny (*Lysimachia nummularia*,

zone 4, sun to part shade), ground-hugging and demure in leaf but possessing enough energy to consume major urban areas. This plant is useful for setting among foundation shrubs, where it can have free reign to ramble at will, filling in and suppressing weed growth. Its golden-leafed cultivar, 'Aurea', is bright and exciting when used with dark foliage, perhaps in combination with bronze or purple ajuga, or at the feet of a purple shrub like Royal Purple smoke bush (*Cotinus coggygria* 'Royal Purple', zone 5, sun to part shade) or purpleleaf sand cherry (*Prunus* x *cistena*, zone 3, sun to part shade).

CLUMPS

Although groundcover plants are frequently thought of as utilitarian and functional, their lowly stature shouldn't detract from their use as ornamentals. Intriguing gardens can be made from low plants in combination with specimen shrubs and trees and boulders of large girth. Clump-forming plants are among the most useful in this circumstance, and contribute an interesting diversity of form and style.

Plantain lily (*Hosta* spp., zone 4, some in sun, most in half shade) is used almost everywhere and has many distinctive species and cultivars. Its dynamic form and spreading stance make it useful for design purposes, and it can be dramatic in presentation when several plants are massed together to form a grouping of their own. Its size range is probably this plant's most distinctive characteristic. It can

Giving directions

Branches, twigs and tendrils of groundcover plants traveling flush to the ground can be directed to where they're most needed. Watch for actively growing branches and adjust them toward areas of bare soil. Very delicate branches of soft green tissue can be anchored with large flexible hair pins. Stronger woody stems can be directed by two short sticks thrust into the ground on each side of the shoot to hold it in place.

Opportunities exist where private property meets public space. The traditional boulevard strip along the sidewalk is often a stretch of neglected grass, but other groundcovering plants can make this vacant space into a garden. For maximum coverage and weed suppression, sweet woodruff (Galium odoratum, zone 4) is used here to thickly carpet the soil, offering dazzling white blooms in spring and green coverage ten months of the year. This space has been made into a public garden, using hostas, grasses, low mugho pines and impatiens combined with inviting seating rocks under the tree.

Ground covers

Watching your step

One of the great advantages of turf grasses is their resilience and tolerance to foot traffic. No other living green surface takes abuse so well. Many ornamental ground covers can be walked on occasionally, yet none can stand up to daily traffic. The solution is to place stepping stones among the groundcover plants to permit safe passage. Or if the plants must be walked on frequently, the best plan is to place the step stones closer together and make an informal "bachelor path" just wide enough for one person. The following ground covers will take a few footsteps, but not too many, or too often.

English daisy, *Bellis perennis,* zone 3
Euonymus spp., zone 5
Chiloe strawberry, *Fragaria chiloensis,* zone 4
English ivy, *Hedera helix,* zone 5
Chameleon plant, *Houttuynia cordata,* zone 6
Creeping jenny, *Lysimachia nummularia,* zone 3
Mint, *Mentha* spp., zone 5
Moss phlox, *Phlox subulata,* zone 4
Mother-of-thyme, *Thymus serpyllum,* zone 3
Ruby cinquefoil, *Potentilla atrosanguinea,* zone 5
Golden pearlwort (Irish moss), *Sagina subulata,* zone 5
Periwinkle, *Vinca minor,* zone 4

Winter value

In cold regions, broadleaf evergreens and coniferous ground covers are important features of winter gardens. They may be the only green foliage in evidence for many long months and so are particularly welcome near entranceways. These are some groundcover plants that have year-round foliage and good winter presence in the garden.

Bog rosemary, *Andromeda polifolia,* zone 5, acid soil
Bearberry, *Arctostaphylos uva-ursi,* zone 1, dry soil
Cotoneaster species and hybrids
Euonymus hybrids
Wintergreen, *Gaultheria procumbens,* zone 4, acid soil
English ivy, *Hedera helix,* hybrids 'Wilson' zone 5, 'Baltic' zone 6
Japanese spurge, *Pachysandra terminalis,* zone 3
Cliff green, *Paxistima canbyi,* zone 2
Periwinkle, *Vinca minor,* zone 4
Juniper hybrids
Russian cypress, *Microbiota decussata,* zone 3

High and dry

Prime territory for groundcover plants is any area of dry shade where nothing else grows. Plants with increased tolerance of low-light, low-moisture conditions still need the basic necessities and always perform better with some irrigation. The following ground covers adapt better to the poverty conditions of low light and inadequate moisture and provide coverage where little else will grow.

Goatsbeard, *Aruncus dioicus,* zone 4
Wild ginger, *Asarum canadense,* zone 4
Barrenwort, *Epimedium* x *rubrum,* zone 5
Wintercreeper euonymus, *Euonymus fortunei* 'Sarcoxie' zone 5
Sweet woodruff, *Galium odoratum,* zone 5
Bigroot geranium, *Geranium macrorrhizum,* zone 4
Herb Robert, *Geranium robertianum,* zone 5
Small Solomon's seal, *Polygonatum biflorum,* zone 4
Bethlehem sage, *Pulmonaria saccharata,* zone 4
Foam flower, *Tiarella cordifolia,* zone 5

be had in tiny 6-inch (15 cm) miniatures or impressive 4-foot (1.2 m) giants. All hostas send up a stalk of lily-like white or mauve flowers, and some are scented, in particular *Hosta plantaginea* 'Royal Standard' and it's double-flowered cousin, 'Aphrodite'. Hostas work well in combination with rambling plants and ferns, and the color range from green to chartreuse to gold to blue to variegations of cream and white is a valuable asset. These plants have a strong design potential, but they also are effective ground covers in the traditional sense.

Violets (*Viola* spp., zone 5, sun to shade) are another clump-forming plant and cottage garden favorite, known in Victorian times as heartsease. The bright and boisterous pansies of spring are weak and impermanent growers in warm seasons, but the smaller species vio-

lets are strong and permanent ground covers in lightly shaded sites. The irrepressible and rampant johnny jump-up (*Viola tri-color*) can jump the bed and riddle itself through the lawn, which is just what some cottage gardeners desire. Better behaved is the northern blue violet (*Viola septentrionalis*, zone 5, sun to half shade), which makes generous heart-shaped leaves and is an abundant ground cover often used as an edging to beds and borders. It spreads by little elongated tubers that are easily pulled out when unwanted. Divisions planted 6 inches (15 cm) apart in spring will form a mass of plants by September.

SPREADING ARCHES

The arching and spreading forms of ground covers are most often low, broadleaf evergreen shrubs and dwarf conifers, both of which have

Out in the mid-day sun

Sometimes enough of a good thing is too much. Strong summer sunlight for more than four hours evaporates a major amount of moisture from leaf surfaces and can exhaust a plant's hydraulic ability to replenish its tissues. Some plants are better equipped than others to stand up under solar abuse and have drought-hardy genes to help them preserve internal moisture. The following plants make a vigorous effort to cover the soil in high-light, low-moisture conditions. But remember, everything requires some water, and the plants will be grateful for irrigation.

Cotoneaster hybrids (low and spreading shrubs)
Donkey-tail spurge, *Euphorbia myrsinites*, zone 5
Bloody cranesbill, *Geranium sanguineum*, zone 4
Evergreen candytuft, *Iberis sempervirens*, zone 4
Juniper species and hybrids (low and spreading shrubs), zone 3
Lavender, *Lavandula angustifolia* and hybrids, zone 5
Creeping lilyturf, *Liriope spicata*, zone 5
Catmint, *Nepeta* x *faassenii*, zone 4
Ozark sundrops, *Onoethera macrocarpa*, zone 3
Shrubby cinquefoil, *Potentilla fruticosa*, zone 2 (low shrub)
Fragrant sumac, *Rhus aromatica* 'Gro-low', zone 4 (low shrub)
Lamb's-ears, *Stachys byzantina*, zone 4

winter interest in cold climates. Their form is a central crown of low, arching branches that spread outward, and some can provide dense coverage when grown in strong sun. Coral beauty cotoneaster (*Cotoneaster dammeri* 'Coral Beauty' zone 4, sun to part shade) and rock spray cotoneaster (*C. horizontalis*, zone 6, sun to part shade) both make thick branches and foliage in bright light, with the added feature of bright red berries. Grown in lower light conditions, they will need a companion carpeting plant such as periwinkle or sweet woodruff under them. Wintercreeper (*Euonymus fortunei* 'Sarcoxie', zone 5, sun to shade) and many of the low groundcover junipers have similar growth habits. Daylily hybrids (*Hemerocallis* hybrids, zone 3, sun to part shade) are excellent ground covers when planted in masses, and can be chosen to span a long season of bloom. They are a combination of clump and arching forms and adapt to many soil conditions.

LOVED BY WOOLLY MAMMOTHS

There was a time in prehistory when the cutting edge in plant material was represented by algae and lichens, capable of anchoring themselves to moist rocks and sucking up water. Their filmy and disk-like forms enabled every cell to get its own drink from the wet stone, but they were without any means of moving water between cells, necessitating a flat, outward growth pattern. Then came ferns. With a primitive vascular apparatus, they could move moisture from one internal place to another and enable cells to build upon each other in all directions. And that was the beginning of plants as we know them.

Walnut wars

Trees of the walnut family take the issue of competition from other species very seriously. Rather than share the bounty, they play a form of chemical hardball, releasing a toxin that poisons other plants within their sphere of influence, thereby eliminating all competition for sunlight, moisture and nutrients. This common method of self-preservation is referred to as allelopathy. In a similar manner, clear-cut land is initially colonized by pioneer weeds that chemically prevent the establishment of second-generation weeds and so open the door to annual and perennial grasses as the succession continues.

Black walnut (*Juglans nigra*), English walnut (*J. regia*) and butternut (*J. cinerea*) all produce the toxin juglone from their roots, bark and foliage. Trying to grow plants, including ground covers, near their root systems can be a frustrating experiment. Some plants are generally tolerant of juglone but may succumb if the dose is too high. Other plants grow for many years with no ill effects. These are some ground covers that have demonstrated tolerance to juglone.

Bugleweed, *Ajuga reptans*, zone 3
Astilbe spp., zone 4
Sweet woodruff, *Galium odoratum*, zone 3
Bloody cranesbill, *Geranium sanguineum*, zone 4
Orange daylily, *Hemerocallis fulva*, zone 3
Showy stonecrop, *Sedum spectabile*, zone 4

Ferns covered much of the earth in moist, shady regions and dinosaurs trod on them with impunity. Fortunately they reproduced well and hung on through the process of natural selection, and the theory is that stray meteors finally eliminated the clumsy fern smashers. Ferns have always been effective groundcover plants and will do much for city gardens, just as they did during the Jurassic period. Their spreading stature is a quick and effective disguise for angular corners and rough, tatty areas.

Royal fern (*Osmunda regalis*, zone 3) is one of the tallest garden ferns, able to reach 4 to 5 feet (1.2 to 1.5 m). Only a few are needed to fill a small area. Ostrich fern (*Matteuccia struthiopteris*, zone 4) grows to 3 to 4 feet (90 to 120 cm) and is a good companion to royal fern, adding a bit of diversity to the height of the grouping. Christmas fern (*Polystichum acrostichoides*, zone 3) is one of a group of evergreen plants; it grows 24 inches (60 cm) tall and provides a good contrast in foliage and winter color. Some fancy-leafed plants will set off the front of a fern groundcover grouping. Japanese painted fern (*Athyrium niponicum* 'Pictum', zone 5) has a distinctive wash of silvery gray over the green fronds, imparting great style, and grows 12 to 18 inches (30 to 45 cm). Maidenhair fern (*Adiantum pedatum*, zone 3) is exquisitely delicate, with trembling lacy fronds and almost invisible wiry black stems. Maidenhair grows 12 to 24 inches (30 to 60 cm) and is a great gem for the very front of a ferny glade.

Ferns will take some sunlight, but not too much, and prefer a setting of light shade with plenty of organic material in the soil and consistent moisture. Provide supplemental irrigation to keep them from drying out in late summer. Plant them around early-spring bulbs that will be in bloom before the trees are in leaf. As the ferns come up, their fronds will hide the ripening bulb foliage.

Vigor unbound

A vigorous nature is appreciated in groundcover plants, but there is abundant vigor and then there is vigor unbound. Some plants have more energy than is required for the gardener's purpose. These are worthwhile ornamental plants of great merit for solving groundcover problems in tough city conditions, but their tendency to spread despite efforts to control and limit growth can cause serious frustration.

Once again, climate affects performance, and what is rampant plant growth in one region may be slow in another. A plant of great usefulness is bishop's weed, also called goutweed and ground elder (*Aegopodium podagraria*, zone 4, sun to shade) in both its pure green and variegated forms. It is an attractive plant, especially in the green-and-white form, suited to problem areas such as chronically dry soil around large tree roots or in a narrow strip running alongside a garage. It must be completely contained or it will quickly travel through an ornamental border and colonize the lawn. The solid green form makes a lovely and sweeping woodland ground cover under a tall tree canopy. Once planted and barely established, it is on the site for all time and can never be successfully removed. With missionary zeal it will pop up yards away from the central planting, spreading the gospel of ground cover at a rapid pace. It should be used for problem areas that defy all other solutions, such as boulevard strips running between the sidewalk and the road and places where maximum-security confinement is achievable. Suitably contained to one area, it will give much pleasure and beauty for a long time.

Virginia creeper (*Parthenocissus quinquefolia*, zone 4, sun to shade) is an extensive woody vine that covers a lot of territory. It will go up, down and over most anything it can wrap its tendrils around and makes a dense covering when allowed to sprawl. Given a flat expanse of vertical bare wall, its adaptive tendrils will develop sticky grips and hang on. In city gardens it will move right down the center of the block, traveling through successive backyards and branching out in all directions to overwhelm the unsuspecting. There is no sense being polite to this vine: it must be clipped back twice a season to keep it within bounds. The vine is the plant of choice for beautifying a chain-link fence with a curtain of large glossy leaves, and it will develop small berries favored by birds. Autumn color is an electrifying scarlet, and it is bare during winter months in cold climates. Virginia creeper should not be confused with its well-behaved and very ornamental cousin silver-vein creeper (*Parthenocissus henryana*, zone 8), which is proportionately smaller and entirely desirable in lightly shady locations.

The interest in ornamental grasses brings many plants with expansive prairie habits into garden use, and some make suitable ground covers. Ribbon grass (*Phalaris arundinacea* var. *picta*, zone 4, sun or shade) has the stylish appearance of fine green-and-white-striped blades about 24 inches (60 cm) high and tolerates wet or dry soil. It can be allowed to expand and cover soil where nothing else will grow. It longs for wide open spaces, so twice a season you will need to cut it back and remove

Keeping weeds out of ground cover

Much of the aesthetic appeal of ground covers is their appearance of uniformity, and it is essential to keep perennial weeds from establishing themselves. Diligent handweeding during the two growing seasons it may take plants to mass together is certainly effective but not often the gardener's first choice. Another method is to put down a 2-inch (5 cm) thickness of organic mulch such as shredded leaves or shredded bark.

A solution that enhances these first graceless years is the use of low-growing annual plants to cover the soil between groundcover plants and provide bloom for the full season. Annual alyssum is a good choice, generous with its flowers from spring to frost and low growing, forming a spreading mat of color. Mini and cascade petunias also sprawl out over the soil and give tremendous numbers of flowers. This is a relatively trouble-free arrangement, requiring only sufficient water and nutrients for the two plantings to share a healthy growing season.

some portion of its roots. Ribbon grass has a typical rhizomatic root system capable of doubling the plant's clump size each year. It will get itself finely enmeshed in other plants and shrubs by marching right through them, and when grown in strong light it seldom can be completely removed. Ribbon grass is another maximum-security candidate and should be confined in some manner, perhaps in a sunken terra-cotta pot.

No list of worthwhile but invasive plants would be complete without mention and warning of crown vetch (*Coronilla varia*, zone 4, sun), a just barely hybridized legume developed for holding back the embankments of transcontinental highways, and a cousin of the lovely, still-wild purple vetchling. This plant was never intended for residential use but somehow found its way into gardening catalogues as a plant solution for dry, infertile soil. Its cheerful pink blossoms have no place in a city garden or any other domestic setting. This creeping spreader needs a slope or prairie of its own to wander around in. The kindest treatment for crown vetch is to drop it from a moving train and hope it finds a suitable place on the embankment.

Meadows: the dream and the reality

Many gardeners have been seduced by meadow-in-a-can seed mixes and their pictures of wildflower meadows dotted with the cheerful blossoms of poppies and daisies. These photos, however, represent just one (probably the best) day in a season and not the consistent state of affairs. The concept of using a meadow as ground cover is a romantic notion that appeals to city gardeners who would like to restore some authentic naturalism to the urban lot. Those are understandable sentiments, but instinct warns it is too easy to be true.

Little is achieved by sprinkling the contents of a meadow-in-a-can over a patch of open ground. Like any kind of seed mix, bed preparation has a lot to do with the success of the planting; and to make a meadow in place of a front lawn requires digging, amending the soil, mulching and removing every scrap of grass plants, forbs (broadleaf weeds) and roots before the seeds go down. The new meadow will need thorough weeding for three years until it is established, although this can be avoided if you devote one entire spring-to-autumn season to "growing out" the weed seeds in the soil and killing them chemically before finally putting down the canned meadow mix the next spring.

Canned seed mixes of this kind make no guarantees that the mix is appropriate for a particular site, or that the seeds contained are even fresh and viable. It is possible to make a custom seed mix by purchasing the various seeds individually. One list of colorful cold-hardy perennial and self-sowing annual ingredients would be white yarrow (*Achillea grandifolia*), red yarrow (*A. millefolium* 'Rubrum'), bird's foot trefoil (*Lotus corniculatus*),

white clover (*Trifolium repens*), basket of gold (*Aurinia saxatilis*), purple pasque flower (*Pulsatilla vulgaris*), California poppy (*Eschscholtzia*) and bluebonnet (*Lupinus sericeus*).

Once established and weed-free, the meadow can be mown to a height of 6 inches (15 cm) in cold climates each autumn, and twice annually (spring and autumn) in warmer regions. Meadows are a transitional stage in the long process of reforestation and are constantly in change. Over three to four years some plants in the mix will become dominant and others will die out. It is possible to add in new plants to broaden the mix when necessary, but you will have more success working with plants rather than seeds at that point.

A low-maintenance arrangement of ornamental grasses, perennials and flowering shrubs makes a drought-hardy and colorful lawn of changing heights and textures. Even in winter the grasses and shrubs continue to give substance and form to this front garden. Grasses are cut down in early spring, fertilizer and mulch are applied, and new growth begins.

Six

Essential maintenance

Change management

Nothing stands still in the garden, unless it's made of cement. Everything grows, becomes established, matures and may even reproduce. These are the hallmarks of successful planting, of soil that is rich with biological life and fertility and of the thoughtful care of a gardener who maintains the landscape. Maintenance activities are the gardener's way of managing change.

Control is a central issue when dealing with city gardens, where space and time are often at a premium. If all leisure time is spent in maintaining control, the moments of restful appreciation may be few and far between. Yet if the garden is let go to pass into a state of chaos, what will there be to enjoy? This is the point where control is tempered by compromise, and decisions are made to attend to certain duties while allowing others to lapse under benign indifference.

The number of maintenance activities taking place is commensurate with the gardener's need for control of change in a landscape that has plans of its own. Manicured gardens may be picture perfect, but obsessive maintenance defeats the purpose of gardening, which is to enhance the naturalism of the landscape. Real life in the plant world is a bit messy, often disorganized and sometimes overtaken by aggressive invasion of uninvited guests. Experience teaches the gardener to strike a bargain with the landscape and establish a level of tolerance. Beyond that point of negotiated growth and chaos, maintenance begins. Failing to establish a zone of tolerance leads only to frustration, exhaustion and the defeatism of gardening with a bad attitude.

There is a wide spectrum of tolerance in housekeeping duties, whether inside or out. Keeping the bed edges sharp and dominating over weed encroachment are individual matters of choice and conscience; one gardener's weed is often another gardener's wildflower. Plants like Johnny-jump-up (*Viola tricolor*) and ox-eye daisy (*Chrysanthemum leucanthemum*) could be welcome colonizers in one garden and doused with herbicide in another. Laid-back meadow lovers may prefer melding drifts of plants to rigid beds with sharp edges; leggy perennials flouncing all across the path have right-of-way in some relaxed gardens.

Essential maintenance is another matter altogether, and has to do with the sustaining functions of moisture, nutrients and pruning. These are the common denominators of all gardening, the basic necessities of healthy plant life that every gardener must deliver to succeed in the natural world. Essential maintenance is what stands between a purposefully planted garden and an abandoned landscape left to its own devices.

Previous page: A hillside can be adapted with terracing to make beds for perennial plants and cascading shrubs, and materials like rough timbers, railway ties or fine finished stone can be used to make the beds. Where the lower retaining wall meets the lawn, a mowing strip of stone or brick carries the mower's wheel and eliminates the need for edging.

Moisture

Going, going, gone

Moisture moves through city soils in strange ways, and sometimes not at all. Modern civilization is heavy footed, and city soils are usually compacted, are low in organic material and humus for water storage and have inferior pore structure for moving moisture through the root zone.

Urban mechanics also work against the best interests of soil quality by efficiently collecting rainwater and removing it from the site. With the purpose of keeping basements dry, modern eavestroughing connected to storm drains has robbed urban soils of vast quantities of moisture. Smart gardeners are now diverting water into rain barrels, an old idea that is new again.

The competition for moisture is fierce in city gardens. The urban forest is a complex collection of plants from several sources. Many plants are installed by municipal governments and private gardeners, but even more are self-sown volunteers. The legions of imported Norway maples (*Acer platanoides*) running riot in urban settings are a testament to biodiversity gone wrong, like the self-sufficient seeding capabilities of many forest giants. Big trees, like all big players, have big appetites. Added to this melange of thirsty plant life are the various wilderness monoliths brought home from vacation retreats as babes in pots, only to quickly assume their true proportions on postage-stamp lots.

The joy of percolation

Despite the many advantages of irrigation systems, natural rainwater is still the best source of the massive volume of water necessary to meet the needs of healthy soil and growing plants. Yet rainwater is increasingly unavailable or erratically in evidence. Either it pounds down in torrents, quickly bypassing the soil and dissipating as runoff, or it fails to appear when most expected. As a result of this inconsistent water supply, gardeners must focus on increasing the porosity of their soil.

The most effective soil structure for receiving moisture is high in spongy humus content, with enough large-particle minerals to ensure steady percolation of moisture through the root zone. The downward trickle, or "perc" movement, is the key to replenishing stores of groundwater accessible to plant roots during drought. Without efficient percolation, root systems would be shallowly clustered near the surface, vulnerable to high soil temperature

and the scorching ultraviolet rays of intense sunlight.

Puddles and standing water that appear after a deluge of summer rain are signs that soil percolation is not working. Irrigation water that runs off into the curb before it can penetrate the soil is another indication that water can't find its way to the root zone. Digging in equal amounts of sharp builder's sand and peat moss will improve both the movement and the storage of water in the top 24 inches (60 cm) of soil. On a lawn, core aeration will open hundreds of holes in the sod, and the mix of sand and peat can be swept into them. Large stone particles like pea gravel dug into compacted soil also establish pathways for water to sink in.

Despite the complexity of this multi-layered tree and shrub border, most essential maintenance takes place in spring and autumn. Storm damage to woody limbs is corrected, but plants are allowed to assume their natural forms. Fertilizing is limited to allowing fallen leaves to return their nutrients to the soil and to occasionally applying composted manure on the soil surface. Weed growth and moisture evaporation are slowed by branches shading the soil. Open areas near the pond are covered by mat-forming groundcover plants, grasses and mulches of sand and pebbles.

Laying weeping tile

If neighboring gardens on higher ground drain into your property, puddling after a downpour and chronically wet soil can result. Or soil can be permanently saturated when an underlying layer of impervious hardpan earth traps water near the surface. Soil amendments won't be enough to solve these drainage problems.

Weeping tile purchased at a building supply center drains water out of the earth and is simple to install. The tile is a flexible 6-inch- wide (15-cm-wide) plastic pipe with perforations along its length and a mesh-cloth covering to keep soil from getting in. Lines of weeping tile can be laid approximately every 10 to 15 feet (3 to 4.5 m), and should lead toward a lower point where drained water can be deposited. Or a French drain can be buried to catch the water. The French drain is a small plastic barrel with holes drilled in the bottom and a place to insert the weeping tile.

- First determine how much area is to be drained and how many lines you will need. A small area may require only one line of tile. Purchase enough linear feet of weeping tile to run the necessary length.

- Dig a trench 10 inches (23 cm) wide and 12 inches (30 cm) deep. If your weeping tile doesn't have a mesh covering, line the trench with landscape fabric. Put 2 inches (5 cm) of large gravel in the trench and lay the tile on top. Fill in the sides with gravel and cover over the top with another 2 inches (5 cm) of gravel. Put 2 (5 cm) inches of soil over the trench and cover with sod.

Delivering water: how much, how often?

Only a completely naturalized landscape allowed to follow its own design with hardy indigenous species, such as meadow weeds and wildflowers, can be assumed to exist and prosper on rainwater alone. Other gardens require a realistic irrigation plan. The amount of water to be supplied each week is relative to the size of plants and their root balls. Trees and shrubs are large structures with significant amounts of leaf surface, and they require sufficient water to wet the depth of the root ball. With too little water, the bottom of the root ball will dry out, and foliage serviced by those roots will drop off. Plants that are grown for their blossoms and fruit require sufficient moisture to manufacture their display. In a season of drought, flowering trees like magnolia will fail to set flower buds for the following season, and apple trees will produce fewer fruits.

Our appreciation of an extended stretch of fine weather often distracts our attention from the rapidly drying soil. Gardeners need to be observant of weather conditions and plant behavior and provide irrigation when soil moisture has noticeably evaporated. The key to effective irrigation of ornamental plantings is to water deeply, ensuring that moisture penetrates the soil to a 10-inch (23 cm) depth. Digging a discrete hole after watering will tell how far down the soil is moistened. Plant roots will not grow into dry soil. Consequently, deep rooting can be achieved only if moisture is available throughout the root zone. Watering for brief periods may moisten only the top inch or two of soil, keeping plant roots shallow and vulnerable to increased soil temperature and drought.

Once crisis conditions occur, it may be impossible to adequately rewet the soil. The stress of overly dry conditions during the growing season can significantly reduce the winter hardiness of herbaceous and woody plants, many of which may suffer considerable twig dieback or die over the winter. Far more plant material is lost to the results of dryness than to insects and diseases. Providing moisture before this crisis occurs can make the difference between healthy robust growth and plants that spiral into permanent decline. The critical point in loss of soil moisture is indicated by dramatic wilt in plants, something no gardener wants to see. If consistent moisture isn't made available at this point, some form of permanent damage can be expected.

A soaker hose system to deliver moisture to the root zone of ornamental plants and shrubs in a slow trickle or drip is a good investment that will last many seasons. In-ground piped watering systems are generally adequate for lawns but not always useful for shrubs and perennial plants. To be effective the spray must pass over the heads of plants. When the spray hits the side of a tall plant, it falls and puddles on one side, leaving the area behind and beyond dry. The soaker hose can be laid under a mulch and remain in place for the entire season or can be moved about as required. Drip systems deliver water slowly and evenly through individual "spaghetti strand" emitters to the base of each plant. They are also useful for large containers.

Smart timing

Wind and sun evaporate moisture very effectively, and attempting to irrigate with airborne water droplets during mid-day can be a futile exercise. Up to 80 percent of the water can be lost to evaporation in the air or on the ground, leaving precious little to penetrate the soil.

The best time to supply water is in the early-morning hours, beginning at dawn, before the sun warms the sky and the wind picks up. This is when plants are least stressed by the environment and will most rapidly absorb what is offered, pumping maximum amounts into their tissues in advance of the day's heat.

Sending a plant into the length of a hot afternoon without a full complement of sustaining moisture is a cruel test of endurance. Major wilting of stems and foliage signals an urgent need for water, and the best method of delivery is to lay down a slowly running hose over the roots and allow water to seep into the soil. This is only an emergency measure, and should be followed up with another deep watering in early evening. Avoid watering after 10 PM, when the combination of wet foliage and lower temperature encourages the growth of disease organisms.

Converting poor devices

Water is delivered effectively when it is supplied at the base of plants with soaker or drip hoses or when it is delivered from overhead to simulate rain. It is least effective when it is propelled in a sideways movement of droplets.

Most garden centers and hardware stores offer a selection of plastic and metal sprinklers that deliver water by various methods of throwing droplets about. Some are inexpensive, and others cost dearly, but most have a common problem: they deliver water from a sideways direction, often at too low a level to clear the heads of vegetation.

These sprinklers may be greatly improved by raising them. If the sprinkler has some form of support bar or molded footing, place it on a low stepstool that won't be harmed by water. Thread a bungee cord through the bar and under the top of the stepstool to secure the sprinkler and connect it up to the hose. This elevated rig can be placed inside a bed for an extended overhead shower, or anywhere permanent in-ground systems won't go.

Getting the feel of it

The purpose of irrigation is to maintain a consistent level of moisture in the soil. When half of the ground moisture has evaporated, that is the point when plants begin to suffer, and also the time to start supplementing water. The unpredictability of weather and the wide variance in soil quality make it impossible to give a calendar date to begin watering. The best method is to examine the soil in several areas of the garden.

Using a hand trowel, scoop up a bit of surface soil and squeeze it into a ball. If it holds together, sufficient moisture is present. If it

This elevated patio and pergola are bordered by a planting of tall grasses that give privacy to the seating area and provide a beautiful show of leaves and tassels all through the winter. Ornamental grasses have the same spreading instincts as their prairie cousins, and runners must be regularly cut back, but grown in a contained box they are only cut down in spring and then left to their own devices.

maintains its shape after gentle prodding with a finger, the soil is overly wet. If it shatters after prodding, irrigation may be necessary soon if rain doesn't come.

Using a spade, dig a small hole 10 inches (23 cm) deep and feel the soil at the bottom. If it is sponge-damp to the touch, groundwater is available to plant roots and the soil's porosity is functioning well. If the soil is completely dry, irrigation is necessary and the soil structure may be compacted.

Making irrigation more effective

Most longtime gardeners are familiar with the contemplative pleasure of standing with a trickling hose in hand and visiting each plant in the twilight of the day. It is generally understood that the gardener also benefits from a sustaining drink and a period of complete privacy — no chat, no glitz, no hustle. These are the moments when the universe is assessed and homicidal thoughts are laid to rest. However, you can effectively reduce the time commitment for watering, as well as the amount of water required, by using traditional xeriscaping methods that focus on preserving soil moisture and preventing evaporation.

"*Xeros*," the Greek word meaning dry, is a reference to the difficulties of maintaining soil moisture in arid climates and seasons. Most gardens have a period of arid weather, and xeriscaping methods can help sustain them between rainy patches. Including drought-hardiness as a primary criterion in plant selection is a smart consideration. This is a simple form of insurance against the possibility of a hot dry season with extremes of heat, when demands on municipal reservoirs may bring about "brown out" water restrictions. Grouping plants together so they can share one area of soil kept moist by irrigation makes economical use of the water supply. Plants grouped together create a micro-climate, shading each other a bit and lowering the surrounding air temperature. The shadows between their leaves and clumps lower the soil temperature, thus relieving stress on root systems.

Amending the soil in the planting hole with water-retentive peat moss or vermiculite (available in large bags from garden centers) will greatly help provide consistent moisture

Saving time and water

Select drought-hardy plants.
Mix damp peat moss or vermiculite into the root zone of plants.
Cover exposed soil with 3 inches (7.5 cm) of organic mulch or 2 inches (5 cm) of stone mulch.
Group plants together in colonies to form an "oasis" micro-climate.
Over-seed lawns in early spring with white clover (*Trifolium repens*).
Allow lawns to go dormant during drought.
Use soaker hoses or drip hoses to water ornamental plants.
Water lawns and plants in the early morning or early evening.

to plant roots. If the peat moss or vermiculite feels dry to the touch, it must first be made wet by mixing it with hot tap water. Dry peat moss, in particular, will not absorb cool water and remains dry even underground.

Exposed soil can be blanketed with a 3-inch-thick (7.5 cm) layer of organic materials to keep moisture from evaporating and to lower the soil temperature in the root zone. Shredded bark or leaves are excellent materials that look and smell good. Pebbles and smooth stones are also effective mulches and complement the appearance of plants. Spread them about 2 inches (5 cm) deep. A stone mulch is permanent, but shredded organic materials will compost in place, feeding the soil with their nutrients, and must be renewed every year or two. Large bark chips are less desirable because of their manufactured appearance and slow, uneven decomposition.

Nutrients

Nature or nurture?

City gardeners sometimes experience an understandable impatience. Surrounded by high-density habitation and overwhelming hard surfaces, they are anxious to get on with quick production. Reaching for the fertilizer is one way to accelerate growth, but at what cost? It is good to remember that for many thousands of years the soil has contained sufficient quantities of these primary minerals (and many essential trace elements) to support healthy plant life and allow the successful evolution of countless plant species. An argument can be made that nature is capable of managing itself. But gardeners often have an urge to nurture the particular object of their desire and may be unable to resist the promise of faster growth and bigger blossoms.

Frequent use of high-potency fertilizers is referred to as pushing plants, or manipulating them to develop at an unnatural pace and with exaggerated features, such as excessive bloom. Pushing perennials sometimes results in plants that flower themselves to death. Forced production of extraordinary numbers of fruit or blossoms means that little energy goes to maintaining other growth functions, and the plant dies from exhaustion. Pushing woody plants often lowers winter-hardiness to dangerous levels by forcing so much new stem growth that no energy goes toward necessary cell hardening. Too much of a good thing can push a plant right over the brink.

Getting in sync with plant cycles

Supplying plants with what they need when they need it is the seasonal dilemma. Patterns of plant growth are complex and varied, and to benefit from supplemental feeding, plants must be ready to grow.

Plant growth is connected to climate cycles, and growing things take their cues from seasonal changes in temperature. Rising temperature causes natural plant hormones, called auxins, to flow and buds to swell. A week of elevated air temperature in late autumn can confuse the cues, and flowering shrubs may unexpectedly break open spring blooms.

Plants benefit from fertilizer only when their auxins are already in production. Always look for signs of new growth, like swelling buds and new shoots, before providing supplemental nutrients. Because of their structure and low-dose concentration, compost and aged manure can be applied at any time.

A spring season with slowly rising air temperature and consistent ground moisture will produce strong root and shoot growth, and this is the optimum time to apply fertilizers. March, April, May and June are key months for feeding plants. Applying fertilizers after July 15 often results in late-season growth that is unable to mature before frost. Lawns benefit from a late-autumn feeding and are the only exception to the July 15 deadline. Southern gardeners can apply fertilizers in late winter for spring crops and gardens and again in early autumn for winter plant production.

Fertilizers can be purchased in organic form or in manufactured formulas of concentrated nutrients. Organic fertilizers are potent enough to produce big blooms on big plants and provide a broad range of essential trace elements (also referred to as micro-nutrients) and soil-building organic material. Manufactured fertilizer formulas provide the three major nutrients (N-P-K, or nitrogen-phosphorus-potassium), but none of the important

Fertilizer schedules, north and south

In the north, provide manufactured fertilizers in March, April, May and June. The last date for applying manufactured nutrients is July 15. Exceptions are compost and aged manure, which can be used at any time, and lawns, which benefit from a late-October feeding.

In the south, provide manufactured fertilizers in January, February, March and April, and again in September and October. Compost and aged manure can be used at any time.

On fertilizers

Essential plant nutrients and some important things they do

A ratio of three numbers (for example, 5-10-10) identifies the percentage of essential plant nutrients contained in fertilizers from either organic or manufactured sources. Ideally none of the numbers should be higher than 15, unless the fertilizer is intended as a one-time-use transplant solution.

Nitrogen: Stimulates chlorophyll production, deep green color, growth of leaves and stems; increases size of plant.
Phosphorus: Influences root growth, bud set and consistent blooming.
Potassium: Strengthens cell structure; builds strong stalks and stems; encourages bud set and disease resistance.

Food for the soil

Feeding the soil with essential nutrients is not difficult. Soil conditioners like sharp sand and leaves improve the soil's tilth and nutrient absorption, making energy readily available. Plant foods from organic sources contain the full complement of important trace elements in addition to healthy amounts of essential nutrients. Some materials like composted manure and leaves are useful in both ways, as conditioners and fertilizers.

Some common organic soil conditioners and plant fertilizers:

Conditioners	*Fertilizers*
leaves	oak leaves (phosphorus, 0.8-9.4-0.1)
composted manure	compost (basic fertilizer, 1-1-1)
peat moss	blood meal (nitrogen, 10-0-0)
vermiculite	bone meal (phosphorus, 1-11-0)
perlite	kelp meal (potassium, 1.5-0.5-2.5)
sharp sand, gravel	wood ash (potassium, 0-1.5-8)
newspaper	coffee grounds (nitrogen, 11-0-0)
sawdust	sheep manure (basic fertilizer, 1.4-1.0-3.0)
gypsum	feather meal (nitrogen, 11-0-0)
compost	fish meal (nitrogen, 5-3-3)

Spring tonic

To encourage vigorous spring growth, manufactured and organic fertilizers in granular form can be used as side dressing along a row or between plants. Look for low numbers, such as:

5-10-5

8-12-6

5-3-8

10-10-10

Designer fertilizer

Gardeners can mix and match organic fertilizer elements to make their own custom planting blend. A handful of this premium mix can be used instead of a manufactured transplant solution when installing new plants or settling divided perennials into their new locations. Various formulas can be put together depending on what ingredients are available, but try to keep the nitrogen element low.
A good designer blend to try is:

1 part blood meal

2 parts bone meal

3 parts kelp meal

4 parts damp peat moss (as a carrier)

Measuring up manure

Well-aged animal manures sold for horticultural purposes are excellent soil fertilizers and conditioners. In too fresh a state, with the scent of their origins about them, they have the potential to burn sensitive roots. But allowed to compost for at least six months or purchased in bags from a nursery, manures are an ideal source of nutrients and biological life. They're all good, but they're not all equal.

Cow manure	0.6-0.2-0.5
Horse manure	1.7-0.7-1.8
Poultry manure	4.0-4.0-2.0
Sheep manure	1.4-1.0-3.0
Swine manure	2.0-1.8-1.8
Worm castings	0.5-0.5-0.3

trace elements, and generally in concentrations high enough to damage plants. The chemical base of nutrients is identical in organic and manufactured fertilizers, but the concentrations, presence of micro-nutrients and humus-making materials differ considerably. The choice is between a balanced nutritional meal and a quick-snack jolt of energy.

Just as many medications are taken only with food, fertilizers should be supplied only in the presence of adequate moisture, never in dry soil. Moisture in soil dissolves fertilizers into a soluble form appropriate for root uptake. When fertilizer is applied to dry soil, its potency isn't diluted by soil moisture and roots are likely to burn. In a dry spring with little rainfall, the big burst of seasonal plant growth will be delayed until the soil is sufficiently wet, and it's best to also withhold fertilizers until rain comes.

Quick fix

Alfalfa is a nitrogen-rich plant often used as a green manure on farm fields. City gardeners can use ground-up alfalfa hay in granular or pellet form to boost soil fertility. Alfalfa contains 5 percent nitrogen and triacontanol, a plant growth stimulant. Sprinkle it generously over a vegetable bed and dig it in, or scatter some in the hole when planting perennials.

You can also make alfalfa tea by soaking 4 cups (1 L) of alfalfa pellets in a gallon (5 L) of water for several hours, and using the tea as a foliage drench. Alfalfa meal is sold in small amounts as an animal feed through pet supply shops. Ask the store to order a large bag for you.

Delivering the goods

Granular fertilizer products sold in bags or boxes are available to plant roots for a longer period as groundwater slowly leaches out their nutrients. Water-soluble preparations are more quickly delivered, but less than 10 percent of the nutrients are absorbed by plant roots. Broadcasting granular fertilizer evenly around perennial plants, shrubs and trees and lightly scratching it into the top inch or two of soil is an effective method of distribution. Compressed granular fertilizer in spike form is very inefficient, as the nutrients are erratically dissolved and distributed. Pressurized injection of liquid fertilizer into soil surrounding tree roots is also an unreliable method of nutrient distribution. If the soil is compacted, fertilizer solutions may remain in one area or drain rapidly away.

High-powered starts

Manufactured fertilizer formulas are available as quick-start transplant solutions for short-term use in establishing new plants or moving old ones. Water-soluble granules with a formula of 10-52-10 supply a large dose of phosphorus to encourage root growth. Liquid concentrate transplant solution has a formula of 5-15-5, and the added ingredient of IBA (indole-butyric acid), a potent hormone to stimulate quick rooting. Either formula can be used twice in spring or mid-summer, initially when the new plant goes into the ground and again about two weeks later.

Organic fertilizers: real food

Most organic fertilizers are less condensed than manufactured ones, contain a full spectrum of the essential nutrients and trace elements and can be used without danger of burning plant roots. These include nitrogen-rich blood meal, phosphorus-rich bone meal, potassium-rich kelp meal and complete-spectrum fertilizers such as compost and aged manure. Other sources of phosphorus are superphosphate (with twice the concentration of bone meal) and triple phosphate (three times the concentration of bone meal); both pack a wallop and can burn plants if not carefully measured. Wood ash is another organic fertilizer rich in potassium. The potassium is rapidly released and sufficiently potent to burn roots. It also raises soil pH, making it more alkaline, and for that reason should be used sparingly on soils over pH 7.5.

Compost and manure can be used generously and in any season. They contain all the primary plant foods and micro-nutrients necessary for strong growth and will keep the soil in good tilth and full of biological life. They can be simply scratched into the soil around plants once or twice during the growing season, or put down as a mulch over root systems. Because their nutrient analysis is proportionally suitable to what plants need to gently spur growth, organic fertilizers can be used at any time in the growing season. These natural foods also contain the full complement of secondary trace elements that are not always present in manufactured fertilizers but are of considerable benefit to plant health.

Nitrogen and perennial plants

Nitrogen has a very strong influence on the growth of perennial plants, causing leaf tissues to swell with moisture and cell walls to become thin and easily bruised. This is an open invitation to disease pathogens and chewing and sucking insects. Nitrogen also causes energy to be directed toward strong vertical growth, making plants gain in size but

Tea in the garden

Drenching infusions of compost or manure tea are quick regenerators for plants at any time. Put a heaping trowel of either compost or manure into a large watering can, fill to the top with water and allow this to sit overnight. Use it the next day to water around plants or as a leaf drench. This is a good way to keep up the energy of plants in full bloom, like roses and dahlias, and can be given each week. Manure or compost tea is a good source of micro-nutrients that plants can absorb through their leaves.

at the expense of bud production and blossoms. Perennials do require sufficient nitrogen for photosynthesis and the manufacture of carbohydrate food, so don't attempt to starve them completely of this important nutrient. But keep the fertilizer numbers low.

Tricks of the trade

Fertilizers manipulate more than growth. Depth of petal color and degree of blossom scent are influenced by the presence of two important micro-nutrients. Trace elements of sulfur and iron can be applied as plants develop in spring and come into bud, producing, for example, roses that will knock more than your socks off. Purchase chelated iron in the fertilizer section of a nursery, dilute it with water according to the package directions and mix in a cup (250 mL) of Epsom salts (containing 13 percent sulfur) for each gallon (4.5 L) of water plus a few drops of liquid dish soap as a sticking agent. Use this solution as a leaf drench every three weeks until buds begin to open. Kelp fertilizer in granular or liquid form also intensifies color.

A tiny garden, only 17 feet wide, makes clever use of every inch designed and built by the gardener's son. The lower walkway is bordered with a long pond running alongside the fence and containing a water jet and fish. The central bed of 'Iceberg' and 'Pink Perpétué' roses conceals another lounge area behind, under the filtered light of a 'Sunburst' locust tree (Gleditsia triacanthos var. inermis, zone 4). Using the deck to make two levels in a small garden creates the impression of greater space and provides a seating area that is always bright. Maintenance is limited to spring pruning of roses and feeding the fish.

Getting the job done

Putting the garden to bed: it's never over

The garden doesn't shut down. Its winter life is as complex as its summer life, just colder. But there is a point when you will want to tidy up and complete tasks in preparation for the indoor wait for spring.

The most important task in autumn is the care and feeding of the soil. This is the time when leaves are plentiful, and as many as possible should be left on the soil surface. Leaves are the best food for all plants and contain many elements that are recycled into nutrients and humus. Shredding or chopping with any kind of mower or machine is all to the good but not entirely necessary. Just spread 2 to 3 inches (5 to 7.5 cm) of leaves on the soil, placing them around the crowns of plants. mall leaves and shredded leaves will stay in place without blowing around. Large leaves, such as those from Norway maples, need to be broken up so they won't mat and cut off air from the soil.

- Perennial plants will appreciate a feeding of aged animal manure or garden compost at this time. Spread it generously over their root systems. Only the lawn should be given a feeding of manufactured fertilizer, using an autumn formula with the last number higher than the others.

- Remove annual plants from the ground and containers once they are blackened by hard frost. The fine-textured roots of plants like impatiens and marigolds can be left in the ground to add organic material, but thick root systems should be removed.

- Cut the stalks of perennial plants down to 2 inches (5 cm), but leave a bit of stubble to identify where they are in spring. Let stalks with ornamental seed heads such as coneflower, astilbe and tall sedum stand through the winter. They make attractive shapes in the snow and also provide seeds to feed winter birds and returning birds in early spring.

- Make sure that all needle evergreens and broadleaf evergreen plants like rhododendron, holly, pieris and euonymus are soaked at their roots before the ground freezes. They need the water to prevent desiccating foliage in winter wind and sun. Broadleaf evergreens in windy locations can be sprayed with an anti-desiccant purchased at the garden center.

- When planting bulbs, be sure to clearly mark their locations with plastic tags. This will prevent slicing up late-blooming tulips and narcissus when you zealously begin turning the soil in early spring.

- Ideally most of your roses are the hardy shrub kind that won't require winter protection. But any tender roses will need to be hilled up with freshly bought soil, piled 8 to 10 inches (20 to 23 cm) high around their crowns. Leave the canes in place until spring, unless they are very tall and may snap in the wind.

- The last thing to do before you settle inside with a good gardening book is to edge all the beds. This sharp defining line will look attractive in the snow all winter, and will give you a neat and tidy beginning in spring.

Pruning

Earning a license

Of all the methods of influencing plant growth, pruning is the most versatile and dynamic. Shaping the form of shrubs and trees directly influences their entire growing future and the pleasure or peril of those who live near them. One distracted moment and thoughtless snip of the pruners and generations of potential blossom, leaf and fruit are eliminated, along with the pleasure they could give. Almost every gardener would be eager for the presence of a bough of magnolia blossom in mid-winter but might eliminate it with a casual pruning gesture in early spring.

Pruning is, first and foremost, a thinking skill. It is important to prune with a reason, to achieve a goal, and not just because the season is right or the blade new and sharp. Pruning requires a special license, or at least a clear statement of purpose. It is a skill requiring much study and deliberation, weighing of methods and choices, projection of possible outcomes. There is little room for indecision or guesswork. It is a very public demonstration of strategy and action, and critics are quick to comment on every cut and snip along the way. Pruning is serious garden business, and it is better to do nothing than to make what amounts to a vulgar gesture with the tree saw.

In limited city circumstances, gardening is full of tough love and tough decisions. The best reason for pruning is to improve the health and beauty of a plant. The worst reason is to alter the form of a plant that is simply disliked. Altering plants that give no pleasure or reward at best makes them less obvious objects of displeasure and, at worst, doesn't make them any more acceptable. This pointless reason for pruning reflects the gardener's inability to make a hard decision. Remove the plant.

When plants are carefully chosen, of appropriate size at maturity for their placement in the landscape and with desirable ornamental features, opportunities for pruning seldom arise. Intelligent choices in plant material eliminate much pruning angst at a later date.

Pruning protocol

Many gardeners are delighted by the discovery of new and shiny hand pruners in their stockings on Christmas morning. So much the better if the item is one of those sleek Swiss blades, slim yet solid in the palm, with lovely oiled springworks and whisper action. And maybe a belt holster, too. Now we are abso-

lutely ready. Trembling by the door, waiting for the opening of pruning season as some wait in the bush for deer, there is a sense that the garden will finally be put right. This season will be different.

In the natural world most pruning is accomplished by wind and ice. But the Swiss have changed all that with those coveted precision clippers, and gardeners now bear the responsibility of using them wisely. An annual assessment of changes in woody plants about the garden is sure to be entertaining and useful. Early spring is the best time to have a look around before plant structures are obscured by leaves. Plants are always up to something.

Storm damage

Shrubs and trees with brittle or weak wood are inclined to split under the force of wind or

This elegant garden entrance requires only occasional clipping of the ground-covering euonymus to keep the path open, and spring pruning for the rose and clematis. Limiting the number of plants lessens maintenance tasks. The trick of the 'less is more' approach is to use minimum plant varieties for maximum punch. Smart gardeners save the bigger plantings, and greater maintenance requirements, for more important areas.

weight of ice. Attending to injuries of this kind should be carried out as soon as possible, regardless of season. Damage can occur during storms, in summer from high wind and lightning strikes, and in winter from wind and ice accumulation.

To fix up ragged damage, remove broken canes and branches that are seriously shattered and hanging by a portion of their wood. Make a smooth and slanted cut just below the damage, leaving as little inner wood exposed as possible. Cracked or cleanly split branches may be tied tightly in place with a soft fabric such as a section of nylon stocking and may eventually heal, but the repair must be checked every six months to ensure the bark doesn't grow over the tie. If the damaged areas are out of reach or sufficiently complicated for more than a simple repair, call a professional arborist.

REMOVING A TREE BRANCH:
WHERE TO CUT
Removing a branch by cutting it flush from the bough leaves a large area of exposed tissue that will take a long time to heal and will offer an opportunity for destructive organisms to invade the inner structure of the tree. Every limb has a branch ring, a slight ridge of wrinkled bark close to where it joins the larger bough or the trunk, and this should be left intact for a healing callus to form. A slight stub remains, but the living tissue of the tree is protected.

Pruning a mature shrub

- Cut out dead branches and twigs, and remove any diseased foliage.

- Remove living branches that cross and rub against other sections of healthy wood, cutting low down on the cane.

- If the interior of the shrub is crowded and dense, thin out the canes and branches that spring from the base of the shrub, removing up to a third of the oldest wood from close to the base.

- Shorten canes only to establish a balanced and natural form.

- Selectively remove small twigs along major branches to allow light and air currents to enter the interior of the shrub.

TO SEAL, OR NOT TO SEAL

Despite the many product choices, tree scientists (dendrologists) are quick to point out that woody plants have effective methods of their own for sealing out pathogens and protecting healthy tissue. Paint and paste preparations are of no value to damaged wood, but perhaps make the gardener feel better. It's actually more interesting to watch wood heal without wound dressing obscuring the action.

Meddling with perfection

Before interfering with the artistic arrangement of woody plants, it's well to understand a bit about the procedure from the plant's perspective. The removal of dead wood, either from environmental damage or disease, goes relatively unnoticed. But a gardener cutting into live wood stirs up quite a hormonal reaction in the plant. Removing a section of a branch on a shrub causes a renewal response and the quick activation of two buds just behind the cut. One section of wood is removed; but responding to the perceived threat to stature, two grow to fill the space. This pattern is likely to work against the gardener's intention of thinning the growth. A better method to reduce mass is to remove the entire branch at the point from which it springs. Removing an entire branch will also stimulate a response, but it is likely to be a new cane rising from the base, and this may be more acceptable. New canes are also easily removed with hand pruners when they are young and tender.

Woody plants have a definite genetic plan that determines what shape and proportion they will achieve with the support of adequate moisture, nutrients and light. Any effort to alter their development in a radical way is likely to cause an unwinnable war and result in plant disfigurement and gardener frustration. The structure and form of woody plants is an expression of their beauty and style, and is enhanced by the opportunity to develop to full size. Only minimal and infrequent pruning should be necessary to emphasize ornamental features. Many ornamental shrubs and trees are available in dwarf form, and this is a good solution where space is limited.

Renovating and rejuvenating

Pruning for appearance is a frequent reason for making alterations in woody plants. In a small garden where shabby plant condition is sure to be noticed, it's essential to remove all dead twigs and foliage and broken or diseased branches from shrubs. This clearing of useless wood can be done at any time. If it leaves older shrubs looking a bit thin and vacant in the middle, this is a good opportunity to grow one of the many forms of clematis vine through the interior structure. The vine will find its way about and provide a perennial display of flowers in unexpected places.

Shrubs that have gone beyond the need for light pruning can be more substantially renovated to renew their form. If the branches rise from a central crown at ground level, begin a three-step process by removing a third of the oldest and thickest canes each spring. Cut them as low down as possible, and the shrub will send up new replacements. Continue the

Famous dwarfs for small spaces

Dwarf American cranberry bush, *Viburnum trilobum* 'Compactum', zone 2, height 5 feet (150 cm)

Trost dwarf birch, *Betula pendula* 'Trost Dwarf', zone 4, height 4 feet (120 cm)

Dwarf burning bush, *Euonymus alatus* 'Compactus', zone 3, height 4 feet (120 cm)

Somerset daphne, *Daphne x burkwoodii* 'Somerset', zone 4, height 2 feet (60 cm)

Dwarf forsythia, *Forsythia* 'Arnold Dwarf', zone 5, height 3 feet (90 cm)

Jeddeloh dwarf hemlock, *Tsuga canadensis* 'Jeddeloh', zone 4, height 5 feet (150 cm)

Dwarf Korean lilac, *Syringa meyeri* 'Palibin', zone 3, height 4 feet (120 cm)

Miniature mock orange, *Philadelphus* 'Miniature Snowflake', zone 4, height 2 feet (60 cm)

Dwarf flowering quince, *Chaenomeles x superba*, zone 5, height 2 feet (60 cm)

Dwarf fragrant viburnum, *Viburnum farreri* 'Nanum', zone 6, height 3 feet (90 cm)

Little Princess spirea, *Spiraea japonica* 'Little Princess', zone 4, height 2 feet (60 cm)

Colorado blue spruce, *Picea pungens* 'Fat Albert', zone 3, height 18 feet (5.4 m)

Bristlecone pine, *Pinus aristata*, zone 2, height 5 feet (150 cm)

Dwarf white pine, *Pinus strobus* 'Nana', zone 3, height 5 feet (150 cm)

Minuet weigela, *Weigela* 'Minuet', zone 4, height 2 feet (60 cm)

Dwarf Arctic willow, *Salix purpurea* 'Nana', zone 4, height 4 feet (120 cm)

next two years to remove a third of the oldest remaining canes, and the shrub will have finally renewed its form and vigor.

Dense shrubs can be carefully thinned to decrease their density without altering height or width. The structural limbs should remain untouched, but remove weak wood and thin twigs carrying foliage to allow light into the interior. The objective should be to see through the plant. Up to one-quarter of the small twigs and leaves can be removed in early summer after the spring growth spurt is finished. Very dense plants like flowering quince and mock orange are greatly improved by thinning their density, and this will also help to divert energy to making more blossoms the following year.

Some woody plants have a tendency to produce excessive numbers of thin suckers (from the roots) or water sprouts (from the bark), usually in response to severe pruning. These have a weedy appearance and divert energy from productive growth and flowering. They can often be seen on lilac, ornamental crab-

A spreading apple tree, showing the history of frequent pruning cuts and shaping, extends its branches as a natural arbor over the pathway from front to back gardens. The close placement of this tree could have been troublesome, but clever management of its structure has turned a potential problem into an asset.

apple and chokecherry. It is possibly a renewal response to the heavy-handed pruning operation of the previous season, and the shoots will need to be removed for the next two or three years. Water sprouts arising along the trunk and limbs should be promptly removed in any season, since they drain productive energy and will never assume a useful purpose. On very young plants, the suckers rising from the root system can be selectively used to develop a permanent framework for the plant. Select one or two for permanent keeping and eliminate the remaining shoots.

Very old plants in need of complete rejuvenation can be severely pruned to generate suckers for the purpose of building new structural wood. Severe pruning can reduce the canes of a 12-foot (3.5 m) shrub to 3 feet (90 cm) of mostly bare wood. Plants renowned for their vigor, such as forsythia and any form of willow or spirea, can be reduced to 12 inches (30 cm). Severe pruning is most successful when plants are grown in at least half a day of bright sunlight to generate energy for renewal. This is one method of saving an heirloom plant variety that may be unavailable commercially.

Standard pruning times

Pruning takes place at different times, depending on what result is desired. However, the times to avoid pruning woody plants are late autumn through late winter. These are the months when cambium cells under the bark are least active and production of wound-healing callus is very slow, allowing pathogens more time and opportunity to enter.

Flowering shrubs form their buds for the

Timely pruning

Summer-flowering plants to prune in early spring

Bottlebrush buckeye, *Aesculus parviflora*
Butterfly bush, *Buddleia davidii*
Cinquefoil, *Potentilla fruticosa*
Elderberry, *Sambucus canadensis*
Flowering currant, *Ribes odoratum*
False spirea, *Sorbaria sorbifolia*
Hydrangea, *Hydrangea arborescens* 'Annabelle' and Peegee hydrangea, *H. paniculata* 'grandiflora'
Roses
Rose of Sharon, *Hibiscus syriacus*
Smokebush, *Cotinus coggygria*
Bumald Spirea (low), *Spiraea* x *bumalda*

Spring-flowering plants to prune immediately after blossoming.

Beauty bush, *Kolkwitzia amabilis*
Bridalwreath spirea, *Spiraea* x *vanhouttei*
Crabapple, *Malus*
Cornelian cherry, *Cornus mas*
Deutzia
Flowering quince, *Chaenomeles*
Forsythia
Honeysuckle, *Lonicera*
Japanese kerria, *Kerria japonica*
Lilac, *Syringa*
Mock orange, *Philadelphus*
Serviceberry, *Amelanchier canadensis*
Viburnum

next year immediately after their flowers fade. Spring-flowering plants such as flowering quince and forsythia bloom on year-old branches grown the previous season. Prune them just as soon as they finish flowering to avoid cutting off next year's buds. Shrubs that bloom in mid- to late summer on new wood grown during the current season, such as hydrangea, crape myrtle, spirea and rose of Sharon, should be pruned immediately after flowering, or in earliest spring before new growth has started and the plant is still dormant.

Woody flowering plants generally sort out into spring and summer blossoming times. Summer-blooming shrubs and trees like smokebush (*Cotinus coggygria*), and elderberry (*Sambucus canadensis*) should be pruned early, before spring growth begins, so that the season's new wood will carry the buds. This rule also applies to roses.

Evergreens can be pruned any time, as long as the wood is not frozen. To keep upward-growing plants like mugho pine at their current size, cut back the candles, or growing tips of new growth, in early summer to thicken their girth without adding height. If a small amount of growth is desired, leave a part of the candle proportionate to the growth desired. Low-growing and spreading plants like groundcover junipers can have their horizontal branches clipped back to a vigorous side shoot. Avoid cutting evergreen plants back to completely bare wood, since it contains few buds and seldom sprouts sufficient new growth.

Deciduous trees are best pruned in mid- to late summer when the leaves are fully developed. Pruning too early (while sap is flowing) often results in heavy bleeding and loss of internal moisture from such trees as birch, elm and maple. Shade trees benefit from thinning their interiors, allowing sunlight and air currents to enter. Small ornamental trees like Japanese maple and flowering dogwood should not have their form altered, and only need to have branches removed where they are rubbing against each other.

Really big blooms

Disbudding is a pruning practice used to make fewer but larger blossoms on plants that produce their flowers on new shoots grown during the current season. Selectively reducing the number of flower buds by a third and leaving the stems untouched directs increased energy to the remaining buds. Peonies, roses and hydrangeas can be manipulated in this way to get very big flowers. Disbudding is often employed by gardeners who want to exhibit overly large blossoms in competitions, and is one of the crucial techniques for growing giant pumpkins!

The patio at the bottom of a terraced hillside garden benefits from artistic shaping of evergreen plants. The euonymus and boxwood hedges have been sheared into geometric forms to accompany individual specimens of Japanese yew, globe cedar and blue-green juniper. Shaping fine-textured conifers into permanent features brings imaginative form and humor to the garden in four seasons.

Peculiar pruning

Considering the elegance and interest of plant forms in the landscape, shearing the foliage of plants to a common flat plane is a very strange thing to do. This method is used to completely obliterate the natural form of a specimen shrub by shaping it as a ball, cube or cone. Over several years, shearing can change a perfectly good boxwood shrub into a squirrel. There is a great deal of shearing to be seen, and most of it quite poorly done so that it has no identifiable shape at all. But as an expression of domination it succeeds just fine. (For more about shearing, see page 131.)

Another peculiar pruning practice is pollarding, the selective cutting back of young branches to the same place every year. Pollarded trees can be kept small and formal with this technique, and each season will sprout new wood with lush and large leaves. The concentration of energy in each new shoot results in a seasonal explosion as the tree's vigor is all directed to these few juvenile growths. Successful pollarding requires a plant with great vigor, such as London plane, northern catalpa, linden, black locust and weeping mulberry. The trees should be fairly young when this practice is started, and annual pruning should take place after leaves fall in late autumn. Young wood can be cut back to the trunk or to a section of a major branch. Eventually a woody knob of stubs and callus forms at the site of cutting. When pollarded trees are in leaf, they are a harrowing form of embellishment to encounter. In winter the history of their severe treatment is bare for all to see.

Artistic management

Espalier is the method of growing woody shrubs and trees horizontally along a wall or fence. It requires great patience, some pruning skill and many years of loving care. But it is a useful and rewarding method of growing large plants in small spaces, and beautiful when successfully carried out. The wall or fence serves as a support and also as protection from wind and cold. Stone walls that accumulate heat are traditionally used for espalier of fruit-producing plants.

Many woody plants can be grown in this manner, but flowering plants and those that produce fruit are most beautiful and interesting. Flowering quince, magnolia and ornamental crabapple are some of the decorative plants used, in addition to the culinary apples, pears, peaches and apricots. Ideally the wall should face south or southwest and the plant must be initially young and flexible.

Cover the wall with a trellis with 6-inch-square (15 cm) windows. Mount the trellis on blocks attached to the wall so that it will stand approximately 3 inches (7.5 cm) from the surface. Loosely tie the plant to the frame with soft fabric. As new, flexible shoots develop, carefully tie them in place or slip them under the frame where possible. Formal designs can be achieved by pruning to produce plants in palmette, cordon and fan shapes on the wall, but the easiest method is simply to carefully space young branches out as they develop in a random pattern.

Maintenance of an espalier includes frequently checking that the ties are not cutting into enlarging branches, and of course providing adequate nutrition and moisture. All branches that resist being tied into the supporting grid or grow too far out from the wall must be cut back to the point they spring from.

Untouchable tops

Never prune the top leader of a tree with the thought that it will help to diminish the size of the plant. Removing the leader will have no effect on inhibiting upward (or apical) growth, but it will open the top of the tree to serious disease and insect infestation.

When a tree's leader is cut or removed, the plant responds by developing a side branch to assume the same role; usually this new branch has a less symmetrical appearance. Trees that are "topped" are often short-lived and debilitated. If the plant is too big for its location, try thinning the interior branches to decrease density or replace it with something of a suitable size.

Forcing flowering branches

Branches of flowering shrubs, ornamental trees and fruit trees can be cut in mid-winter and forced into bloom indoors as a prelude to the real thing later in spring. Cut branches with obvious buds any time after the beginning of February. Split the lower tips of the branches, or crush them lightly with a hammer, and stand them in water in a cool, shaded place for twenty-four hours. Then bring them into a warm, bright room, perhaps near a window, and watch as the buds swell and open over a period of two to four weeks. Plants good for forcing include forsythia, flowering quince, redbud, flowering dogwood, magnolia, apple, cherry, apricot and pear.

Seasonal Summary

Spring

Start summer-blooming bulbs indoors in pots
Clean up winter debris, twigs and damaged limbs
Rake through thatch and dead grass from lawns
Remove evergreen boughs from perennial plants and
  emerging bulbs
Cut back stalks of perennials and ornamental grasses
Edge beds
Set peony hoops in place
Prune roses, removing dead and spindly wood
Feed roses and perennials with organic fertilizers
Feed bulbs with balanced granular fertilizer
Prune summer blooming shrubs like hydrangea,
  butterfly bush, rose of Sharon
Thin overgrown shrubs with crowded branches
Turn compost and add some manure to start it
  working
Plant perennials, shrubs, vines and trees
Remove as many small weeds as possible before
  they get big
Cut back foliage of spring bulbs when half brown
Plant annuals

Summer

Prune spring-flowering shrubs like lilac and forsythia
  immediately after blooming is finished
Stake tall plants and thick perennial clumps where
  necessary
Trim conifers to control growth
Fertilize lawns, shrubs and trees
Mulch lawns with peat, compost, manure
Keep up deadheading annual and perennial plants
Dig out large weeds
Prune roses lightly to encourage late bloom
Fertilize roses with granular rose food
Feed annuals every three weeks with water-soluble
  fertilizer
Provide water to large woody plants during drought
Take photographs
Plan the fall bulb order

Autumn

Dig and prepare new beds for spring planting
Renovate old beds and borders
Divide perennials
Move woody plants
Plant new perennials, shrubs and trees
Plant spring bulbs and cover with leaves or
  evergreen boughs
Remove annual plants
Lift and store tender summer-blooming bulbs after
  the first hard frost
Distribute finished compost
Core aerate lawns
Sow grass seed
Dig out large weeds
Edge beds
Fertilize lawns between October 29 and November 5
Plant bare-root roses
Mulch beds and borders with two to three inches of
  shredded leaves
Cut back perennial plant stalks to three inches
Water conifers deeply in November just before the
  ground freezes
Gently tie loose conifers like cedar to prevent snow
  damage

Winter

Mulch newly planted perennials with evergreen
  boughs after the ground has frozen to prevent
  winter heaving
Collect seed and plant catalogues
Take a gardening course
Review last season's pictures
Plan annual plants for spring
Prune wisteria and grapes in late winter

Afterword

Black thumbs

There is no dispute regarding the fact that humans were born into a green world. The garden came first, and Eden was a naturalized setting of indigenous plants already highly evolved through natural selection. Humanity made a living of gardening or farming for thousands of years. But history is organic and always changing, and only recently has the old reliance on the earth and its natural processes been eclipsed by industry and technology. Gardening is no longer a basic life skill, but for many it is a weekend recreation or a creative outlet. And for others it is a therapeutic refuge, settling the nerves and renewing the energy for nine-to-five workdays.

Some people profess to have a "black thumb," or an inability to make anything grow. This is not true, their thumbs are perfectly normal. But their confidence has been eroded by long separation from the gardening life and the basic information of how plants grow and reward the gardener. Gardening is based on learned information and acquired skills, and requires absolutely no special instinct. The necessary investment is time, and everyone has the same twenty-four hours each day. How the hours are spent is what makes the difference between black thumbs and gardeners.

There is a certain amount of apprehension at the beginning of every new venture, and gardening is a very big venture, indeed — as big as the world we live in. But thankfully, gardening mistakes are forgivable. We learn from them and move on with improved competence. Beginning in a small way, with a window box or small corner, is as relevant and important as moving mountains. What counts is making any kind of beginning, in any season, and getting on with it. Now is probably a good time.

*The author's favorite spot in autumn, a meeting place for birds surrounded by the overwhelming pinkness of obedient plant (*Physostegia virginiana *'Vivid', zone 2), stonecrop (*Sedum spectabile *'Autumn Joy', zone 2) and self-seeded cosmos and cleome.*

Hardiness zones

When writing about plants, I have tried to include the northernmost climate zone where they are reliably hardy. But it is an horticulturalist's frustration to deal with three different, and conflicting, zone maps commonly used in North America. Inevitable contradictions are sure to arise, and the best indicator of plant hardiness is this: if nurseries in your region offer a plant for sale, it is safe to presume the tree, shrub or perennial will be winter-hardy. Common sense is a valuable guideline in gardening.

Finding your hardiness zone

Winter-hardiness is influenced by several factors. Genetic inheritance of cold tolerance, soil moisture, depth of snow coverage, wind exposure, and local micro-climate all affect winter survival of plants. Hardiness zones are based on the average minimum winter temperature in each region. Plants with your hardiness zone number or lower should reliably withstand winter conditions.

Zone	°F	°C
1	below −50	below −46
2	−50 to −40	−46 to −40
3	−40 to −30	−40 to −34
4	−30 to −20	−34 to −29
5	−20 to −10	−29 to −23
6	−10 to 0	−23 to −18
7	0 to 10	−18 to −12
8	10 to 20	−12 to −7
9	20 to 30	−7 to −1
10	30 to 40	−1 to 4

Index